From the President's Address to Congress on the End of the Gulf War Wednesday, March 6, 1991

" ... the brave men and women of Desert Storm accomplished more than even they may realize. They set out to confront an enemy abroad, and in the process, they transformed a nation at home.

"Think of the way they went about their mission — with confidence and quiet pride. Think about their sense of duty, about all they taught us, about our values, about ourselves. . . .

"The America we saw in Desert Storm was first-class talent. . . .

"In a very real sense, this victory belongs to them, to the privates and the pilots, to the sergeants and the supply officers, to the men and women in the machines, and the men and women who made them work. It belongs to the regulars, to the Reserves, to the National Guard. This victory belongs to the finest fighting force this nation has ever known in its history."

— President George Bush

☆ DESERT ☆ WARRIORS

The Men and Women Who Won the Gulf War

By the Staff of  USA TODAY

POCKET BOOKS

New York   London   Toronto   Sydney   Tokyo   Singapore

An *Original* publication of Pocket Books

 POCKET BOOKS, a division of Simon & Schuster Inc.
1230 Avenue of the Americas, New York, NY 10020

Copyright © 1991 by Gannett Satellite Information Network, Inc.
Cover photo copyright © 1991 by Superstock

ISBN: 0-671-74875-0

First Pocket Books printing May 1991

10 9 8 7 6 5 4 3 2 1

POCKET and colophon are registered trademarks of
Simon & Schuster Inc.

Printed in the U.S.A.

Contents

Preface

The men and women who won the Persian Gulf war were ordinary people asked to do extraordinary things.

They did their jobs, their duty. And they did them well.

Like the F-15 pilot who flew in the first wave of sorties into Iraq. The female helicopter pilot who died. The tank crew member who was wounded and got the Purple Heart. The radio DJ who entertained the troops.

They were all tested in ways they never expected. And they passed with flying colors, inspiring a nation that had mounting domestic worries.

This is the story of those Desert Warriors.

Here are tales of war seen through the eyes of the soldiers, through their letters home and their words on the battlefront. We try to tell you a little about each of the more than 300 soldiers who died.

Much of what you'll read appeared in USA TODAY. From Jan. 7, 1991, through March 6, 1991, stories about the war dominated the Nation's Newspaper.

The stories of these soldiers are sometimes sad, always inspirational. Many will linger in your mind for a long time. We are proud to share their stories with you.

— Peter S. Prichard, Editor, USA TODAY

GULF WAR NUMBERS

Costs of the conflict half a world away:

U.S. troops in gulf at height of war: 540,000

U.S. troops killed: 322

Where troops died: 136 in combat, 186 other

U.S. troops killed during Desert Storm: 214

U.S. troops wounded: 339

U.S. troops still missing in action: 10

U.S. POWs released by Iraqis: 21

Total allied air sorties flown: 116,000+

U.S. aircraft and helicopters lost: 57

Allied aircraft lost during the war: 11

Planes Iraq claims it has shot down: 180

Estimated Iraqi troops killed: 50,000 to 100,000

Iraqi POWs held by allied forces: 62,000+

Iraqi tanks destroyed or captured: 3,700

Iraqi armored vehicles neutralized: 2,400

Iraqi artillery pieces destroyed or captured: 2,600

Iraqi aircraft and helicopters destroyed: 123

Iraqi planes escaped to Iran: 137

Scuds launched at Israel, gulf countries: 81

White House estimate of cost: $69.5 billion

Projected U.S. share: $15 billion

Pledged by allies: $50 billion

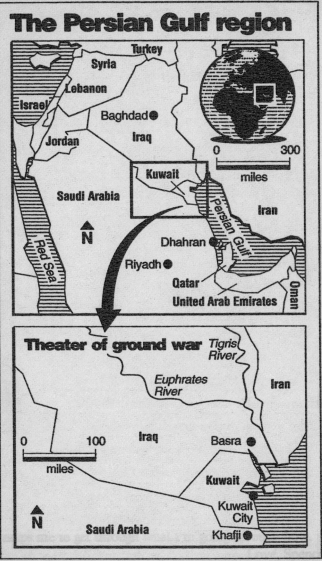

The Persian Gulf region

Turkey
Syria
Lebanon
Israel
Jordan
Baghdad●
Iraq
Kuwait
Saudi Arabia
Persian Gulf
Iran
Dhahran●
Riyadh●
Qatar
United Arab Emirates
Oman
Red Sea
N

0 ___ 300
miles

Theater of ground war

Tigris River
Euphrates River
Iran
0 ___ 100
miles
Iraq
Basra ●
Kuwait
Kuwait City
N
Saudi Arabia
Khafji ●

Source: USA TODAY research   By Marty Baumann, USA TODAY

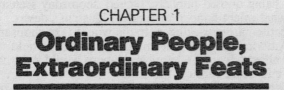

CHAPTER 1

Ordinary People, Extraordinary Feats

The Persian Gulf war began with the futuristic glow of missiles over Baghdad, and ended 43 days later as wars often do — with soldiers trudging through sand and mud to victory. What happened in between is the story told in this book.

It's been called the first live TV war, the first computer war, the first hot war of the post-Cold War era. It was also the first real war for a generation of Americans — men, women, volunteers and reservists — who remembered only the mire of Vietnam.

Thousands of images remain from Operation Desert Storm: Laser-guided bombs diving neatly down air shafts; POWs staring wide-eyed through swollen, bloodied faces; F-15s screaming off the desert floor in wave after relentless wave; the arc of Patriot missiles intercepting blind-flying Scuds.

And finally, hundreds of Iraqi soldiers, then thousands, raising their arms in surrender. Some kissing their captors. Others giving themselves up to reporters armed only with notebooks. A new image of a victorious America loomed larger with each dispatch from the front; the memories of Vietnam were being replaced.

Easy, then, to forget how it had begun, with questions

like this one from 9-year-old Christopher Key at Fort Campbell, Ky., one week before the war: "What if everyone else's dad comes home," he asked quietly, "and my dad doesn't?"

Not just families feared the war. Congress, world leaders, analysts, even some administration officials, when not being quoted publicly, offered doomsday scenarios of what might happen in Saddam Hussein's desert.

Battle-hardened, dug-in Iraqis would take thousands of American lives. A half-million Iraqi mines would stall any allied advance. Chemical weapons would swirl nausea and death through the lines.

Others predicted another Vietnam — another protracted, no-win war. And, there was the two-decade sense that America's technology, like the space shuttle *Challenger,* was faulty and weak; that America had lost its leading place in the world as an economic and military power; that America couldn't cut it; that it didn't have what it takes to win.

On that first night of the war, Jan. 16, 1991, a grim-faced President Bush told the nation that "the liberation of Kuwait has begun."

What followed was a new kind of war. It was the stunning debut for high-tech weaponry that cost billions, and worked. It was commanded by a new breed of military leaders who handled the media as adroitly as they commanded their troops. And it was fought by a highly motivated volunteer force of 540,000, neighbors and friends from across America, including women joining men near the front.

The Persian Gulf war changed America as much as it changed the map of Middle East politics. A new American image resulted, one that may endure long after the last rusted hulks of tanks and artillery are cleared from the deserts of Iraq and Kuwait.

"Baghdad was lit up"

Just before dawn on the first day of war, at a secret air base in Saudi Arabia, F-15 fighter jets roared off runways and headed north. Every 14 seconds. Like a string of lights in the moonless Arabian night, they took off for the first raid on Baghdad.

The pilots throttled up, climbing to escort a squad of Stealth fighter-bombers. The fighters easily broke the sound barrier. Waves of sonic explosions pounded the desert floor, where platoons of Marines raised fists and cheered.

The strikes were precise, thunderous, all but stopping the world as they were broadcast live on television.

"There's anti-aircraft fire going off right now," shouted reporter Don Kirk while dictating a story from Baghdad. "I'm getting the hell off the phone. ... I'm going ... Bye."

"Baghdad was lit up like a Christmas tree," said one of the first pilots over Iraq, Air Force Lt. Col. George Walton of San Antonio, Texas, leader of the 561st Tactical Fighter Squadron. His F-4G Wild Weasel carried missiles to knock out radar systems for enemy surface-to-air missiles. Walton said he saw one anti-aircraft missile, adding it was "far away."

Resistance was to be light, almost inconsequential for most of the air war, but no one knew what the Iraqis might be concealing in the haze of cloud cover on that first morning.

"There was a lot of stuff being thrown at us — just about everything and the kitchen sink was coming up through the clouds," said Air National Guard Capt. Thorne Ambrose, 36, of Columbia, S.C., flying his first combat mission. "There were smoke trails in the blue sky above us where some of the SAMs [surface-to-air missiles], were going. I saw one go straight up behind me, straight up in the sky, and blow up. We were up in the target area probably for 10 or 15 minutes. It just seemed like time stood still."

"It was the most scary thing I've done in my life," said Flight Lt. Ian Long, a 31-year-old Tornado pilot in Britain's Royal Air Force. "We went in low over the target — as low as we dared. We dropped the bombs and ran like hell. It was absolutely terrifying. There is no other word for it. We were frightened of failure, frightened of dying."

The air power was awesome: Each F-15 carried 12 tons of bombs; they skimmed over the ground at treetop level and could strike an enemy aircraft 100 miles away; sitting in the cockpit was like sitting astride a rocket.

The first air kill was credited to Steve Tate, a 28-year-old Air Force captain from Watersmeet, Mich., who fired a single Sparrow missile at an Iraqi Mirage fighter.

The air fighters did not fight alone, however.

As jets moved north toward their targets, help came from the sea. The rumble of Tomahawk cruise missiles shuddered the decks of the battleship USS *Wisconsin* off the coast of Kuwait. Headed for Baghdad and the presidential palace 250 miles away, this would be the missile's first use in warfare. The *Wisconsin* fired 10 of the first 100 cruise missiles.

Sailors watched in awe as the missiles growled and stammered in the air, appearing to falter for a moment, until computer chips kicked in. Then they were off on a terrain-hugging run, each casting a yellowish halo along the waves. "It was pretty to see them go off," Fireman Apprentice Anthony Husser, a pink-cheeked 19-year-old, said simply.

"There was no time for fear," said Boatswain's Mate 2nd Class Timothy Kollman, 27, of Bay Shore, Long Island. "A charge went through your body."

Over the ship's speakers came the terse words of Capt.

David S. Bill III, 47, the *Wisconsin*'s commander. "All the cards are falling into place," he told his 1,500 crew members. He read a cable from Vice Adm. Stanley Arthur, commander of naval forces in the gulf. It ended with a quotation from James Michener's novel *The Bridges at Toko-Ri*: "Where did we get such men?"

"Where, indeed," Bill added.

That was how the war began. Only one U.S. pilot, Navy Lt. Cmdr. Michael S. Speicher, 33, of Jacksonville, Fla., was lost that first morning. He left a wife, a 3-year-old daughter and an infant son.

"We thought she'd be safe"

Iraq retaliated — but not with the feared land offensive, nor with chemical weapons. On the second night of the war, 10 Soviet-made Scud missiles were fired at Israel and Saudi Arabia. Seven Israelis were slightly injured.

"We must destroy Saddam," vowed Uzi Mothede, 20, who roused his family before one of the first Scuds fell 100 yards from his home in Tel Aviv. "I saw a bright red light. It was the missile. The glass broke in our house. A clock above the window flew into the kitchen. Then a great cloud of dust came from where the missile hit and it filled our house and I thought, 'Oh God, this is the chemical.'"

No chemical weaponry ever fell, but life in Israel would never be the same. "I never thought I'd need the gas mask. It was still in the brown box," wrote reporter Richard Price in Jerusalem. "Then the air-raid siren went off. My first reaction was: 'I'm totally amazed. It's happening.' I intend to carry this mask with me from here on. Everywhere."

In all, 81 Scuds were fired at Israel and Saudi Arabia. They failed to pull Israel into the war as Saddam had hoped. The Iraqi Scuds were clumsy at 40 feet long and heavy at 3,000 pounds, relatively inaccurate, and easily intercepted by Patriot defenses.

The U.S. Patriot anti-missile system had been criticized as costly and needless during the Reagan administration. But the sleek 18-foot Scud-busters — at a cost of $1 million apiece — were inanimate heroes. Fired most often in pairs, the Patriot would arc and twist into the black sky, leaving looping trails of light.

At posts throughout Saudi Arabia and Israel, soldiers trained in the mathematics of trajectories and intercepts, and conversant in computer science, launched Patriots with heart-stopping precision, sometimes only seconds before Scud impact.

Army 1st Lt. Quinton McCorvey of Pensacola, Fla., and his two battery mates chalked up two Scud kills early on. "Last night took me quite high," McCorvey said of shooting down a Scud.

But the Scud would still give U.S. troops their bloodiest day of the war.

On Feb. 25, part of a Scud missile, apparently disintegrating in flight after a Patriot hit, fell randomly onto a metal barracks housing U.S. reservists at al-Khobar, just outside the main base in Dhahran, Saudi Arabia. A virtual direct hit, it killed 28 soldiers. It was a water-purification unit — troops who never expected to find themselves as a target.

Among the dead was Spec. Christine Mayes, a 22-year-old University of Pennsylvania student from Rochester Mills, Pa. She had been in the gulf only five days, and had been engaged to David Fairbanks the day she left for the war. Her parents had tied a yellow ribbon to the lone birch in the yard of their wood-frame, single-story home.

Her parents wrote later, "She died for what she believed in. She was proud to be an American." Said her sister, Candi Mazuirki, "We thought she'd be safe so far from the action."

"Put fear in your back pocket"

For 40 days and 40 nights, the allied pilots rained 142,000 tons of bombs on Iraq and occupied Kuwait — about 5 percent of the total ammunition dropped during the years of World War II. They flew more than 116,000 sorties.

Four out of five bombing runs hit their mark. The precision bore a political price. A hardened bunker, used by women and children as a shelter and believed to house an Iraqi command center, was attacked by Stealth bombers Feb. 13. Pictures of the heavy casualty toll, the first real images of death, were used by Saddam in the following days as a propaganda tool.

Around the world, hopes for peace soared and fell as Iraq, obviously looking for a way out, tried to cut a face-saving deal with the Soviet Union.

But Kuwaiti oil fields were spewing black smoke over hundreds of miles; reports of atrocities in the capital city were growing. And President Bush had already given Gen. H. Norman Schwarzkopf, commander of the allied forces, a date for the ground war. "G-Day" was to be Feb. 23.

It was the onset of what many thought would be a bloody, gruesome fight against an entrenched enemy. Still ahead lay the largest minefield in the world — the "Saddam Line" between Kuwait and Saudi Arabia. Still unknown was how many of Saddam's Republican Guard troops had survived the initial bombardment, or how hard they'd fight.

No one knew then that within five days, U.S. Marines would be driving through the downtown streets of Kuwait City.

Bravo Company, a unit in the Army's 3rd Armored Division near the Saudi-Kuwaiti border, expected the worst. In the opening hours of the ground assault, 140 "grunts" turned grimy faces upward to hear the words of Capt. Keith George. His voice was softer than he wanted, and he fidgeted, kicking up the cinnamon-colored sand.

"By the end of February," he told his troops, "you will be advancing under live fire against targets that shoot back. Everybody, from commanders to the lowest private, is going to be scared. I've never had real bullets fired at me, either. Everyone is feeling the same thing. Everyone has the same fear factor. Be a man and reach down and put that fear into your back pocket."

After 30 minutes, George mopped his brow. The men headed off to dinner, more silent than before.

The "Hail Mary"

The battle plan to beat the Iraqi army was simple: "We're going to cut it off and then we're going to kill it," explained Gen. Colin Powell, head of the Joint Chiefs of Staff.

Pacing in his Riyadh command center, Schwarzkopf coolly assessed the air assault. He knew Iraqis were dug into coastal positions, bracing for an amphibious attack by 17,000 U.S. Marines aboard ships off the coast. The Iraqis were also led to expect an attack across the southern border between Kuwait and Iraq.

It was time for what Schwarzkopf called his "Hail Mary" offense, sending some of his troops deep into Iraq.

The allies would indeed strike boldly across the "Saddam Line," blasting away minefields and plowing a virtual highway into the heart of Iraqi defenders. The amphibious assault would never come, but the threat would nonetheless distract Iraqi defenses.

At the same time, U.S., British and French forces on the ground would sweep westward and then unexpectedly head north into Iraq. In a final blow, they would encircle the enemy and move in for the kill.

With amazing ease, the 1st and 2nd Marine divisions rolled across Iraqi defenses in the south. The 101st Airborne Division and its more than 300 attack helicopters began the move to outflank Iraq to the west. Speed was essential.

To reach Kuwait, the 1st Marine Division would need to cross two fortified obstacle belts, and confront as many as 12 Iraqi divisions. Air power would help, Lt. Col. Jim Heidrich told his troops before the attack. "The good news is that the odds are only 11 to 1, instead of 12 to 1," he deadpanned.

But the 1st Marine Division broke through Iraqi lines with relative ease. Fearsome defenses were not there; reconnaissance teams had found gaps in the minefields; some Iraqi prisoners even helped the Marines mark off minefields. The division thundered 60 miles in three days, destroying 500 Iraqi armored vehicles and capturing 7,000 prisoners before reaching Kuwait City. Division casualties: five dead, 29 wounded.

"If you can get around behind somebody, they collapse pretty quickly," said Maj. Gen. James M. "Mike" Myatt. "I didn't want to slug it out with every tank and infantryman we came across. I wasn't interested in destroying the Iraqis. I wanted to defeat them."

Most U.S. soldiers never needed to fire their weapons; they drove in convoys into Kuwait. "This has been a cakewalk," said Col. Ted Reid, commander of the 197th Brigade of Fort Benning, Ga.

Their low death toll was "almost miraculous," Schwarzkopf said. But he added, "It will never be miraculous to the families of those people."

Comrades died, leaving only names to be carved into granite memorials in towns with names like Willow Grove, Pa., and Whitehouse, Texas. A total of 332 Americans died or are missing: 214 in Operation Desert

Storm; the rest before the air war began. According to initial reports, only 28 died in the actual ground war. Among those killed by allied firepower — the ironically named "friendly fire" — was Marine Cpl. Dion Stephenson, 22. He left his home in Bountiful, Utah, to serve in the military, just as his brother had, and their father before them. He carried a snapshot of him and his father standing alongside Arnold Schwarzenegger. "It doesn't change a thing," said his father, James Stephenson, of his son's death. "He's still a hero."

Lance Cpl. Troy Moseley, 21, of Snyder, Texas, went to the gulf prepared to see a lot of death. He volunteered for a Marine unit charged with graves registration — the task of identifying troops killed in action. "The unsung heroes of this damn war" is how their commander, Brig. Gen. Charles C. Krulack, described them.

For Army Maj. Robert Williams, war was haunting. "I killed my first man today," said the former West Point ethics professor, who was commanding a tank battalion. "I'm not sure I feel very good about it."

Daughters at war

This was a war fought by the oldest, best-educated American army in history. Tens of thousands of soldiers were reservists and National Guards members — many middle-aged — called up from their regular jobs in offices, factories, hospitals, law firms and universities across the country. It was a volunteer army, highly trained and computer savvy. A handful were Vietnam veterans. The average age was 27; 93 percent were high school graduates.

In charge was "Stormin' Norman" Schwarzkopf, who preferred the nickname "The Bear," and combined a quick temper with an IQ of 170. Schwarzkopf, 57, a veteran of two tours in Vietnam, was only a year away from retiring in relative obscurity. Instead, he would walk away with credit for one of the nation's greatest military campaigns. Schwarzkopf was admired by his troops. He was an infantry soldier — he walked and talked as one more comfortable in the battlefield than the corridors of political influence.

Different, too, were the forces under his command. The biggest difference from the armies of the past — a phenomenon once unthinkable — was that one in 16 soldiers in the war was a woman. The Air Force called the gulf war "the biggest concentration and employment of women in combat situations" in U.S. history. Women comprise 11 percent of the total 2 million U.S. troops. In the gulf, they made up 6 percent of the 540,000 troops deployed.

For every one who entered combat as an infantryman, fighter pilot or battleship sailor, six others were assigned to tend their wounds, bring them mail, supply them the necessities of war — fuel, water, food and ammunition.

This is where the women served: behind the lines in logistics bases, above the battlefield, piloting tanker jets refueling bombers on their runs, at sea directing air control systems or inside the battle lines flying Chinook helicopters used to move troops and Iraqi POWs.

Like their male counterparts, they would die, be taken prisoner, exult in victory. In the Persian Gulf, unlike in Panama or Grenada, the front lines were blurred. "It used to be that if you were in the rear with the gear you knew you were safe," said Marine Maj. Sue Flores. "Is there 'a rear with the gear' in Saudi Arabia? I don't think so."

In addition to air missions that placed them close to enemy fire, women were never out of range of Iraqi missiles and artillery. "Our grandfathers and fathers who served in wars before us never expected their granddaughters and daughters to be in combat," said Army

Spec. Diamond Schiffers, 20, of Slidell, La. "It's hard to accept. But this is a test for us — a chance to prove we can do this and anything else."

Spec. Melissa Rathbun-Nealy, a 20-year-old Army truck driver from Newaygo, Mich., was among the 21 POWs captured by the Iraquis. Also captured from a downed Chinook helicopter: Army Maj. Rhonda Cornum, a 36-year-old flight surgeon.

"My God, I feel it's one of the happiest days in my life," her father, Donald Scott of Buffalo, N.Y., said after his daughter, Rhonda, was released.

Maj. Marie Rossi, a helicopter pilot, wasn't so lucky. Her helicopter crashed near its Saudi base as she returned from one of dozens of re-supply missions. Her death came only hours after a cease-fire had been announced.

One of a handful of women at the front lines during the ground attack on southern Iraq, Rossi, 33, of Oradell, N.J., flew the big CH-47 Chinook helicopter — the pack mule of the war. She led Company B, a unit of pilots from the 159th Aviation Battalion at Fort Stewart, Ga., dropping equipment and paratroopers deep inside Iraq.

"What I am doing is no greater or less than the man who is flying next to me," Rossi said before her death. "Or in back of me," she added, jokingly.

"Thank you, Americans"

The final march into Kuwait City on Feb. 26 came without air support because the smoke from 550 burning oil fields was too thick to fly through. On the ground, 6 million barrels of oil were ablaze each day. The fumes made it difficult to breathe. The roar of the infernos made it difficult to hear. "This is like driving into hell," said Capt. Ed Ray as the 1st Marine Division crossed the last 30 miles to Kuwait International Airport.

The troops met only scattered resistance. Kuwaiti troops entered first, to retake their capital city. Americans and other allies soon followed.

Kuwaitis took to the streets in a celebration of freedom that lasted all day and into the night.

"Thank you. Thank you. Thank you, Americans," said Issam Sharif, a 28-year-old Kuwaiti bookkeeper.

There was talk of changing the name of Baghdad Road to George Bush Road. Almost everyone was obsessed with the thought of seeing the president, touching him.

"I want to marry him!" screamed Kaleh Mahammed, a 25-year-old teacher who was dancing in the streets. "I want to kiss him, I want to hug him, I want to send him beautiful cards. I love him."

"Who would have thought this could happen to an American in the Mideast?" said Lt. Col. D. Andy Setzer of Arlington, Va., as he handed out autographs to dozens of Kuwaiti women and posed for a battery of pictures.

Kuwait, though, was devastated. Hundreds of burned-out cars, tanks, trucks, motorcycles and vans littered the roads and desert spaces. Streets had been dug up, leaving huge piles of asphalt scattered across the landscape. Dozens of oil pipelines had been cut and blocked highways into town. There was no electricity, no phone system and, in one of the world's richest oil states, limited gasoline. Kuwaitis had been tortured and killed.

Homes were looted, universities destroyed.

Most horrifying were the attacks on the Kuwaiti resistance, the members of which were systematically hunted down, tortured and killed.

U.S. Ambassador Edward "Skip" Gnehm returned to fill the post he was named to a year before. He joined Kuwaiti Health Minister Abdula Hab al-Fawvan on a postwar visit to Sabah hospital. They saw wounded resistance fighters, Iraqi prisoners, a boy hurt stepping on a mine and 21 bodies in a morgue. "This just demonstrates how bad it really was," Gnehm said.

"There is not a family in this country that doesn't have a story," Fawvan said.

'It's still in my head'

The end of the war meant new beginnings for the troops who served in the gulf. At home, Bush's popularity soared to a record 91 approval rating percent after peace was declared. In Washington, there was talk of a political future for Schwarzkopf, the gruff, smiling strategist; and also for Powell, the first black and, at 53, the youngest officer to lead the nation's military.

Homecomings for soldiers began March 8. Amid the tears and hugs, memories pressed close.

"I've taken so much for granted," said Army Sgt. Michael Green. "I'd be happy to be stuck in traffic. It'd be wonderful if I went to my driveway, and my car wouldn't start. That all sounds great now."

Few were ready to share the grimmer moments. "I don't think I'll ever be the same old happy-go-lucky person," said Army Spec. Jim Randall, 28, of Chicago, Ill. "There's this new ugliness in me because of what I saw and did."

Army Spec. Norman Francis, 24, of Youngstown, Ohio, said he'll never shake the memories of pulling bodies from the the Scud attack in Dhahran that killed 28, including two close friends. "All I can think of is those guys I used to play basketball with laying there asleep in their sleeping bags. Except they weren't sleeping, they were dead," he said. "It's still in my head."

Army Spec. Vince Egyed, 33, of Detroit, spoke for many of the troops as they prepared for the long journey home. "I keep thinking about the fragileness of life, how close you can be to dying," he said. "Those of us who are going home are real lucky, but we're not the same."

CHAPTER 2
Letters Home

During the war, mail became the yellow ribbon that bound the Saudi desert to America.

Letters were addressed to family members, friends, and just "any soldier." Each military person received an average of 18 pieces of mail every week.

Families shared some of the letters sent back to them from the gulf with USA TODAY. These excerpts take you to the desert — to its fear, bravery and loneliness. In these letters, America's service men and women speak for themselves.

Jonathan Erin DuBray, 26, airman third class aboard the USS Eisenhower — *to his mother, Donna Robbins, of Jacksonville, Fla.*

Dear Mom,   August 9

So I guess you're worried about my situation, and so am I.

If for some reason I don't come home, to you I leave everything. Please take care of Brittany [his baby daughter]. I have made no will, so I hope this letter is sufficient. I will sign this letter with my legal name. I don't have much to give, but what there is, is yours. Please don't be too upset. This is just in case. Hope for the best and pray for peace.

All my love, Jonathan Erin DuBray

(Airman DuBray came home safely in September when the Eisenhower was rotated stateside.)

■

Carl R. Davis, 30, corporal in the the 3rd Battalion, 9th Marines — to his mother, Jennie Davis, of Minden, La.

Mama: August 22

I got an idea. You know whatever you send me, I share it with my less fortunate buddies. If you send me four razors, I'll probably give two away. That's the way we are trained to be — as one. I was thinking maybe you could get the church behind you. I would see to it that everything gets handed out fair. I mean, I don't get that much mail, but some of these Marines get nothing. One Marine before we left bought a cassette tape designed to reduce stress. Kind of an easy-listening tape. We pass it around. It helps us relax. Some of those would help.

Your son, Randy

(When his request was published in USA TODAY, Randy started getting a huge volume of mail. Packages came from three countries, from prison inmates, from kindergarten classes and nursing homes. Randy became a celebrity in the battalion — a truck was sent to get his mail. He made sure everything was distributed and that thank-yous were written. When ground war neared, he asked his mom to thank people and tell them he couldn't write because they weren't allowed paper anymore.)

Kelly R. Smith, 24, a Navy aviation ordnance man 2nd class aboard the USS Saratoga — to his wife, Lynn, of Atlantic Beach, Fla.

Hey Babe,   August 23

I should come home with a couple more ribbons, although I think it's the wives and girlfriends who are the real heroes. You have to put up with the frustration of not knowing. I try to tell you everything, but by the time you receive my letters, the press had already had it out on the 6 o'clock news. . . . Before you know it, all of this will be over.

With all of my love, Kelly

■

Capt. James Schreiner, 31, an Air Force fighter pilot — to his parents, Mary and Herb Sutcliffe, of Oakland, Md.

Dear Mom and Dad,   August 24

We are housed in an air-conditioned building, but it is quite crowded. The food is not bad, considering. It is cooked by Indians or Pakistanis and the main dish is some kind of curry. We get chicken, but they take the chicken and chop it up into pieces — bones and all. We also get something like coleslaw without the slaw; it's just chopped-up lettuce.

After a long flight, a nice cold beer would taste good. But the Saudis don't believe in alcohol. . . . Yesterday, I went on a sortie (a flight mission) and the temperature outside was 120 degrees. We had to put on a flight suit, helmet, mask, etc. Although the plane is air-conditioned, it takes about 45 minutes to get the plane cool. Next week, we expect to go up more often. Please forward all of my mail, especially magazines. Even junk mail.

Love, Jimmy

John Evans, Jr., 24, an Army second lieutenant and helicopter pilot — to his parents, Carolyn and John Evans, and grandmother Martha Evans, of Greensboro, N.C.

Dear Mom, Dad and everyone,   August 26

Well, the biggest thing I've been fighting is boredom. We are now playing the big waiting game. I hope we can reach a peaceful resolution to this whole thing, but if we can't, we're prepared to kick his ass. Sorry, Mom.

I love you and miss you, John

■

Michael Barkley, 22, a senior airman with the U.S. Air Force — to his mother, Carolyn Kabler, of La Grange, Ky.

Dear Mom,   August 28

Well, here I am. Saudi Arabia! It's really not that bad. The weather is great and the Saudis are nice. They take a little getting used to, though. They've got lots of weird customs and are easily offended, so you have to be careful all the time. You can't use your left hand for grabbing or touching things because they consider your left hand "dirty" so they freak out when you use it. All we're doing is sleeping and eating and waiting for "the word." No one knows what's going to happen, but we're ready for it.

I love you, Mike

■

John Marks, 25, an Air Force first lieutenant and pilot — to his parents, Albert and Mary Marks, sister Angie and brother Joe, of Overland Park, Kan. With his partner, Marks flew his A-10 Warthog to destroy 23 Iraqi tanks in one day of flying, believed to tie a gulf war record.

Dear Mom, Dad, Joe and Angie,   September 1

Arrived here in Saudi yesterday, and I thought we had flown to another planet. I really can't describe how desolate it is. No trees. No rocks. No bushes. No life of any kind. The "sand" really is more like a fine cement-mix powder, almost white. The war hasn't started yet, and hopefully won't at all. It's bad enough without people shooting at you. Send cookies, please.

Love, John

(John was deluged with packages. Church members wrote when his address was published in their bulletin and school kids adopted him as a pen pal. One package held a Saddam doll with detachable limbs made by his sister, complete with green uniform and mustache. He told her the guys had fun tossing it around and, after the cease-fire, they re-attached the arms of the doll held up over its head in a gesture of surrender.)

■

Gerald L. Stevens, 32, Army 82nd Airborne Division — to his mother, Lois DeNobrega, of Hagerstown, Md.

Dear family,   September 3

You are in my thoughts. I am doing pretty good. My biggest concern is not knowing when we are coming home. Otherwise, everything else is tolerable and sometimes actually enjoyable. It's almost 1 a.m., and I'm out back keeping a guy company who is on radio watch. We are both writing letters and, to our amazement, we are enjoying a cool breeze wafting through the air. That's a first for us since we have been here. I am pretty safe and we are landing more and more troops and equipment every day. Don't worry about me, worry about the Iraqis. U.S.A. ALL THE WAY!!

Love, Jer

Connie Anderson, 25, an Army first lieutenant and nurse assigned to the 47th Army Field Hospital in Bahrain — to her family in Colton, Ore.

Dear Mom, Dad and family,   September 4

I have died and gone to Hell!! I don't think anything could be as bad as this place is. We are in the middle of the desert but right on the beach. The water (Persian Gulf) is beautiful; blue, clear and filled with raw sewage. Our tents are set on a big sand dune and they have no floors, so we live on and under a layer of sand. Our tent has 16 women in it smashed together. Today, the tent was 112 degrees on the inside. The water we drink is so hot it tastes like bath water. The women's bathroom consists of two boxes with three holes apiece. This is for 130 women. Pray every day that I will be home soon. I don't think it will help, but it can't hurt.

Bye for now, Connie

■

Pvt. John H. Mackey, 20, a tank loader with the 24th Mechanized Infantry — to his mother, Geraldine Mackey, of Marietta, Ohio.

Dear Mom,   September 5

How is everything back home in WONDERFUL, BEAUTIFUL, STUPENDOUS, GREAT OHIO? You could probably tell by my last sentence how it is here. I'm just listening to Aerosmith. Tapes are the only things that keep me sane. ... DEAR poochy bear Mom, could you please mail me some AA batteries?

Love, John

Jason Gardner, 21, a corporal in the Marines — to his girlfriend, Trish Mendoza, of Chatsworth, Calif.

Hey gorgeous,   September 7

I'm not doing so hot. We're working round the clock so I haven't gotten any sleep for the past couple of days. I haven't even had the chance to eat, so I'm having stomach cramps. Plus, we're having a lot of sand storms. It gets so bad that it seems like night. About every three words, I have to wipe off the sand from the paper. ...

Love ya, Jason

■

Jeff Hall, Army specialist — to his mother, Carol Mattison, of Tucson, Ariz.

Dear Mom and family,

I got to go to the PX today. I had to wait in line outside for over an hour. Once we got in pretty much all of the good stuff was taken up, like batteries, shower shoes and greeting cards. I just bought a watch. ... Well, my bills are finally being forwarded to me. You know the bill collectors can always find you.

Love, Jeff

■

Sean Walters, 25, is a private with the Army's 101st Airborne. This letter was sent to his parents, Ric and Betty Walters, of Osseo, Minn.

Dear Mr. and Mrs. Walters,   September 7

My name is 2nd Lt. Gregory E. Otis and I am your son's platoon leader. I wanted to write and try to ease some of your worries. Right now, the biggest enemy your son is facing is the heat. ... The platoon is living in tents, and although living areas are a bit cramped, the soldiers are getting plenty of rest. Pfc. Walters is my driver. . . . "Walt" (as everyone calls him) is invaluable. I rely on him heavily and he carries his load without failure.

Gregory E. Otis

■

Dean Hodgson, 19, a private first class serving with the Army 82nd Airborne medic unit — to his mother, Dotti, and father LaVonne, of Santa Maria, Calif.

To Mom and Dad,   September 8

I am doing OK, but it still sucks here in Saudi. We are getting pretty bored. People are making bowling balls and pins out of water bottles. Also they make footballs out of water bottles and tape. Oh, guess what, someone stole my book of Mormon. Can you believe that? I really hope I just lost it. Mom, thanks for all the letters, please keep them coming. Also thank you for the beef jerky.

Love, Dean

(Dotti Hodgson, Dean's mother, calls the response to the publication of Dean's letter in USA TODAY "phenomenal." He got dozens of letters from all over the country. An elderly woman from Maine said she made the best chocolate chip cookies in the world, which she'd send if he would write her. He did, and she did. The mail also brought nine books of Mormon to replace the one lost.)

■

Jason Steere, 20, a private in the Army's 82nd Airborne — to his brother, Matt Steere, 17, of Sioux Falls, S.D.

Matt,   September 15

Don't worry! I'm just on a little vacation. I went to the

beach — a big beach where you can't see the ocean. And all the women left for college and the beer sold out. Well, okay, it's not quite the beach. But I'm fine.

Love ya, Jason

■

Larry McJunkin, a master sergeant with the 24th Infantry Division — to his brother, Curt McJunkin of Apple Valley, Minn.

Dear Curt and family,   September 16

So far in our battalion, two people have been bitten by scorpions and one by a sand viper on his way to the shower. All my folks now wear boots to the shower.

Love, Larry

■

Marine Staff Sgt. Eddy Johnson, 27 — to his uncle, Larry Winters, of Saginaw, Mich.

Dear Larry,   September 19

Congress and senators came for a dog and pony show. CBS has interviewed us twice; CNN is here and *Newsweek*. It's all a crock. We get a shower every 14 days. You get one day off in the rear. Those guys in the aft Army got it made, four-man rooms with air-conditioning. This is the hardest work I've ever done.

We always move at night. We carry loaded weapons. We've had some accidental discharges. Two hurt pretty bad, one stomach with 9mm and one leg with 16mm. I hate sand bags; we dig out our bunkers and holes every day. The wind fills them up two to three feet. It's a battle in itself. At least if we fight, the enemy can't hide here.

SEMPER FI, Eddy

Sgt. Thomas Dyson, 24, of the 1st Marine Division — to his parents, Kathy and Ed Dyson, of Hollis Center, Maine.

Dear Mom and Dad,   September 22

Quick note as I eat dinner, if you still have the MREs (meals, ready to eat) I gave you, go ahead and eat them. Don't eat anything with chicken, though. They are generally good, but some of the chicken has gone bad. Dysentery has hit a lot of guys to varying degrees. One guy was hospitalized for a day. I wasn't nearly that bad, just unhappy for 48 hours.

Keeping my head down, Your loving son, Tom

(Ed Dyson ate one MRE his son sent. "It wasn't bad. There was fruit cocktail, beef and gravy and pound cake. My wife wouldn't have anything to do with it, though." One of their son's mail requests was for Pepto-Bismol.)

■

Mark "Beaker" Davis, 82nd Airborne Division, gun loader for a M-155A1 Sheridan light tank — to his girlfriend, Cindy.

Dearest Cindy,   September 23

I just wanted to say I love you with all my heart and I hope to be in your arms soon! I am out here sitting on my tank and looking at your picture. I hope you are getting my letters and please tell everybody I send my love and keep the letters coming!

Love you forever and sweet dreams, Beaker

Robert Holland — to his wife, Theresa, in Fayetteville, N.C.

Dear Theresa,

Hi Sweetheart. I miss you very much.

Your love is very special to me. I wish words on a paper could talk out so you could hear the tone of my voice when I say "I love you." You mean the world to me, and I give you my word that I will be home to you.

Every day over here gives me time to think and look over our marriage, and I can say in my heart that I can't live without you. You are my reason for living.
Love ya, Poo Poo.

From your husband, Boo Boo, always

■

Rob Collins, a first sergeant with the 3rd Battalion, 11th Marines — to his girlfriend, Trish Wrilshxer, of San Fernando Valley, Calif.

Dear Trish,   September 25

This desert living sucks. The Army and Air Force live in barracks with AC. The Marines live under nets in the sand in the desert. That is why the Marines always get the job done, they are miserable and want to go home. The only thing in Saudi we have seen is sand, desert, heat, scorpions, snakes and flies. This place is ugly. Trish, you would really hate it. The people are very weird.

Love, Rob

Corporal Sharon Foster, 22, is a medic with the HHC 241 ID/Division. This letter was written to her son, 17-month-old Cedric Foster II, who was being kept by her parents, Gertha and Billy Ramey, in Calumet Park, Ill. Her husband, Cedric, 22, was also a medic serving in Saudi Arabia.

Dear Puddy-Pie,   September 25

How are you doing, baby? Mommy misses you so much, but I can't come home just yet. Daddy and Mommy have a job to complete, and we'll be home as soon as it's finished. We're in Saudi Arabia standing ground for what we believe in, so things will be a little easier on you when you grow up. Not a day goes by where I don't call your name, picture your little face or yearn to hold you tight in my loving mother's arms. So have grandma help you say your prayers for our safe return home.

                                        Love, Mommy

(During the war, the grandparents read all of the parents' letters to Cedric, Jr. He grabbed their picture, kissed and held it. The USO provided a video of the couple, which he watched every day before breakfast.)

■

William Marsh, 28, a radio operator with the 101st Airborne — to his mother, Elizabeth Marsh, of Loveland, Ohio.

Dear Mom,   September 26

It's Dead Zone time. That time during the day when it's just too hot to do anything; so we stay inside our rented Bedouin tents and sweat. I drink about eight liters a day of water to keep from dehydrating. Bottled water comes to us every day from the Saudis. We wrap the bottles in cloth and soak them in water to keep the bottle and the water in it cool; drinking hot water makes me sick. We wear boxer shorts or nothing beneath our heavy cotton polyester uniforms, that's to prevent crotch rot, and we use powder to prevent lice and crabs. The breeze almost makes it feel cool, when, in fact, it sucks the perspiration off so fast that your skin feels dry so you don't think you're sweating until it's too late and you're dehydrated.

We spend time writing letters we won't get answered for a month, hauling water, filling sandbags, cleaning our equipment and complaining. We have live rounds which make us drunk with the idea of using them; and we have our protective (gas) masks on at all times which keeps us sober. All our meals come from little foil pouches that we heat by throwing out on the ground — works better than a microwave.

We anxiously await going home or going to war.

And as the crisis escalates, even more deeper probing brings only more questions: Can I handle the emotional stress of watching my friends die? Can I handle the physical stress of trying to save them? Do I have the courage? Can I take a life? Will I fight or will I run? Am I prepared to give my life so that others may live free?

I love you, Bill

■

John David Schrank, 21, a petty officer second class aboard the USS John F. Kennedy *— to his mother, Grace Schrank, of Oak Creek, Wis.*

Hi Mom, September 27

We almost went to war today. We had an Iraqi ship that wouldn't stop. What happened was they're stopping all ships checking them for oil, weapons and etc. Well the ship wouldn't stop, so we launched our alert birds, with cluster bombs and laser guided bombs, plus we launched two SEAL teams. I thought for sure this was it. Then a shell was shot about 50 feet in front of the Iraqi ship and that is all it took. The ship stopped and it was boarded. What it sounds to us is one big game. They test us, we test them. We threaten them and they threaten us, but we always win. We have so much power out here I can't explain it all. It really is exciting when the pace picks up. Aircraft everywhere, live weapons and war planes catapulted every two to five seconds . . . Well that's all I've been doing.

God bless you, John David

■

Dwight Williams, an Army helicopter pilot — to his mother, Anna, of Tallahassee, Fla.

Dear Mom,   September 30

The sun rises without warning. One minute total darkness; the next, the sky is so bright your eyes hurt. The wind starts shifting, and you can smell the the latrines on the other side of the compound. One good thing about the smell is it attracts the flies so they leave you alone. Of course, when you go to the latrine . . .

My buddy Matt and I have a war going on between us. The practical jokes are getting better and better — I just sewed the cuffs in his pants together. The other day, I swapped his flight suit with another guy's. Matt's a real big guy and the other suit was a small. My cockpit work has increased dramatically here. It's amazing how a pilot reacts to the lack of flying. He gets very irritable. . . . But as soon as he goes flying, it's like a junkie finally getting his fix. I couldn't imagine doing anything else for a living but flying. . . .

What's hardest on most of the people here is that no one really knows when something is going to happen.

Love, Dwight

Edward Ledford, 26, a helicopter pilot with the 101st Airborne — to his mother, Evelyn Ledford, of Asheville, N.C.

Dear Mom: September 30

Well, another day in Paradise! My morale and motivation are high. Since arriving here we have been sleeping in a parking garage of an airport that is under construction out here in the desert. ... My company collected money and went into the city and bought each of us a comfortable chair that upgraded life 100 percent. We have built several tables, a Ping-Pong table for recreation and other stuff. We have all the water we want to drink, showers and outhouses that aren't really all that bad. The heat has not been a problem at all. Sure we sweat, but I sweat back in the States.

I love you, Eddie

■

Marine Lance Cpl. Terry Robinson, 21 — to his fiancee, Brenda Holiday of Belleview, Fla.

Dearest Brenda,   October 4

The desert ain't no joke! There's no trees, no bushes and no shade. We had nomads and some of Oman's military watching almost everything we did. We also saw a bunch of camels, donkeys and jackals (something like a wolf). We also found a lot of dead animal skeletons. By the way, we found a camel skull and I got one of the teeth out for a souvenir. I'll be sending it to you shortly so you can pack it away with the rest of my things (if you would, please).

Loving you always, your future husband, Terry

(Shirley Robinson, mother of Cpl. Robinson, says, "The family banded together and bombarded him with mail."

He requested ice cream and his mother found dehydrated ice cream. He wrote his fiancee almost daily. Terry and Brenda, who have been dating for nine years, met at church and plan to get married in the fall. Brenda keeps the camel tooth she received in a souvenir collection box.)

■

Doug O'Brien, 21, an Army field artillery specialist — to his fiancee, Valerie Kopacki, of Baltimore, Md. Their wedding date was planned for April 27, 1991.

Dear Val,   October 12

We're at our base camp in the desert. We're 45 minutes from Kuwait. We are the front line U.S. troops.

This place sucks. It's hot as hell. This place is full of flies and scorpions and it stinks like camel shit. The time I spend over here is going to be the most miserable time of my life. I wish I could be with you now. I don't know when I will get to make a phone call. They said we're only coming out of the desert every 4 to 6 weeks.

I love you, Doug

(Valerie wrote Doug every day, often sending him the things he asked for: tapes (UB40, Johnny Gill, the B-52s), cartridges for his Nintendo Gameboy, Reese's Peanut Butter Cups, potato chips, tuna, sardines and playing cards. She says she hopes Doug will be home by their wedding day, but hasn't heard for sure. Meanwhile, she waits to go ice skating again. That's how they first met 4 years ago. Skating alone, she says, reminds her too much of him and their separation.)

Larry Gross, 22, a mortarman in the Army's 82nd Airborne Division — to his brother, Todd "Tater" Gross of Carlinville, Ill.

Dear Tater,   October 12

While we were in the field two Arab children came over to the mortar pit. They brought a sandwich and cold water for us. We traded some American money for Arab money. Here it is. They wanted our American flag to wave but all we had were patches so we gave them one of those. It kinda made it worthwhile, us being here, that is. One said "Saddam Hussein" and pointed to our mortar cannon, used the hand to simulate an explosion. We died laughing. They have a satellite phone set up over here now. I'm going to try to sneak a call in some night. You can only talk 5 minutes but it's better than nothing. . . .

Love you, Larry

(Gross was able to call home Christmas Eve and speak to his mom, Joanne Scott, who wrote him every day. Todd Gross received the Saudi money — two coins and two bills.)

■

William S. "Spence" Jackson Jr., 21, a lance corporal with the 2nd Marine Division — to his mother and father, Clara and William Jackson, of Hartford, Conn.

Dear Mom and Dad,

Continue to pray for me. Don't worry.

Tell Doll [Darlene, his sister] . . . I'm looking forward to her wedding [scheduled for Aug. 31, 1991]. Ask Rev. McKnight [pastor at his church, Old Ship of Zion Baptist Church in Hartford, Connecticut] to remember me in prayer. Thank you for bringing me up the way you did. It helps me to get through what I'm going through now.

Love, Spence

(Every Sunday, Spence and others related to the 300-member Old Ship of Zion Baptist Church are remembered in prayers. He has been a member all his life.

When he first arrived in the gulf, Spence asked to be sent various things including washcloths, socks and skin cleanser. Later, he asked for stationery, and "absolutely anything to eat.")

■

1st Lt. Don Barlow, 25, with the Maintenance Battalion of the Army's 197th Infantry Brigade — to his parents, Don and Bobbie Barlow, of Raleigh, N.C.

Dear folks,   October 14

It's a beautiful Sunday morning. Wind and temp are very comfortable. Just returned from church — we built our own church out of Bedouin tents and wooden crates. Really feels like a Sunday. We've been trying to normalize things and get the troops back to the days of the week. Sunday is a day of rest and of sports. Good break for the guys. Each company in turn takes one other day off during the week.

War always captivated me with a sense of romanticism and glamour. Understandable when the closest I ever have been to it is by way of books or John Wayne. However, when you sit so close to it and you have time to let your imagination run wild, reality sets in.

I know why I am here and am very proud to be a part of this time in history — first-hand. I just hope that Americans all over don't root for war like the way they cheer on the favorite football team. This isn't a game — life out here is harsh and war would be hell.

Love, Don

Thomas Oltorik, 29, a Marine captain and F-18 pilot — to his brother, Dennis; sister-in-law, Shelley; nephew, Ross; and dog, Czar, of Cincinnati, Ohio.

Dear Dennis, Shelley, Ross, Czar,   October 16

We continue to fly CAP [combat air patrol] missions over the Gulf of Kuwait — 24 hours a day, seven days a week — as a show of force and for security of Navy ships. Not much happens on those trips. . . .

The "local" Arabs we've trained with are nice guys overall and have a good sense of humor, but they don't go to the bar on Friday nights and kick back a few cold ones with their buds! Talked to some guys who have met the Kuwaiti fighter pilots who brought their 20 or so A-4's and F-1's to Saudi after the invasion. Apparently these guys took off on short notice [after] the Iraqi attack and, in the course of a few hours, managed to kill 20-plus Iraqi helicopters with heat-seeking missiles, drop bombs on tank columns, come back, get a fresh reload, go out again — and do the same thing until their bases were overrun and then fly their jets to Saudi. That's pretty admirable. . . .

Funny thing now is that these Kuwaiti pilots in exile want to plan and go on their own mission into Kuwait right now!! They're saying, "We want to go now and bomb Iraqi troops." They don't care if we go along or not! They are apparently very fired up. They would need a lot of support to survive a strike like that, but they don't seem to care. I'd like to meet one of these guys and buy him a drink (a soda!) . . .

Love, Tom

Leveius Bryant, a specialist in the Army — to his mother, Ella Bryant, of Garrison, Texas.

Hey,   October 26

Things here are about the same, hot in the day and not too cool at night. As for the way we sleep . . . you find a spot on the ground with the scorpions and snakes. See, we sleep on this pad that you have to blow up. And it being sort of cool at night, the snakes try and find some heat. Since the air bag holds in hot air, the snakes go for it. The other morning, I woke up with two curled up right by my head. I've gotten used to it now.

Love ya, Leveius

■

Chuck Whittlesey, Marine chemical warfare officer to the fifth-grade class at Cherry Crest School in Bellevue, Wash.

Dear children of Barbara Inman's class,   October 29

Today I received one of the nicest gifts any person could ever want — I got your envelopes full of letters, pictures, poems, leaves and love! I have shared it all with my mates. You know what? I am from Bellevue, Wash. I came in the Marine Corps in 1967 from Bellevue and will return home next year. I am 42 years old, married and have one daughter (13 years old).

I am a chemical warfare officer. My family lives on Okinawa, Japan, right now — that is where I was stationed before I came here. I hope to be a school teacher in the Bellevue school district when I come home. I want to teach 5th grade. We are very tired and dirty all the time. We spend all of our time preparing to fight. I need to tell you that no one wants to fight but someone needs to know how. Our home sounds as wonderful as when I last was there. The leaves you sent brought tears to my eyes.

You children are the most beautiful and precious things on earth. What you see and learn will help make our world a more peaceful and wonderful place. Thank you for the time and effort you spent to show your respect for me and my mates.

Your friend, Chuck Whittlesey

■

Army Capt. Michelle Perna, 24, had her resignation papers on the desk of her commander on Aug. 2, when Iraq invaded Kuwait. She was sent to the gulf as a transport officer with the 507th Support Group. What follows is a letter to her husband, George Albertini, Jr., in Washington, D.C.

Dear George,   January 11

I want to tell you all there is to tell, but I can't because it is all classified. I know quite a lot of information, on what our mission is and where and what we plan to do. I never imagined in my wildest dreams that I'd be part of an operation like this. And to think that people had a problem with women going into combat. Well, I'm no different than the actual combat troops, in so many words. I just never imagined I'd be doing some of the things I'd be doing.

All my love, Michelle

(Michelle called George in March and said she planned to be home in July, almost a year since she left for the gulf. George says when she arrives, "We plan to get away somewhere and get reacquainted.")

Sgt. Denise Lynn Bushong, 27, of Army Chemical Intelligence — to her mother, Barbara Bushong, of Lafayette, Ind.

Mom,   January 17

(2:45 a.m.) The war has started. I have been listening to the news from the get-go. I stood here and watched a squadron of fighter jets (F-15s) take off from the airport here. Mom, I love you and everyone in my family. I want all of you to be strong. I am fine over here. Really, I'm OK. I will stay strong because I have a promise to uphold — I promised my family I would come home.

Love you all, Denise

■

Sgt. Thomas Dyson, 24, 1st Marine Division in Saudi Arabia — to his parents, Ed and Kathy Dyson, of Hollis Center, Maine.

Dear Mom and Dad,   January 18

I got your tape yesterday, the first day of the war. First to the war and then to your letter. The war came as a bit of a surprise, we were asleep. We didn't know until we heard it on the news. That sounds bad, but we didn't need to know and it's had no effect on our daily routine. Actually, there are a couple of changes. The helicopters fly A LOT lower — safer that way. The planes fly higher. Mail will slow to a trickle. . . . We'll live. So far, it looks pretty good.

Love, Tom

■

Capt. Kevin Walker, 27, of the Army's XVIII Airborne Corps Artillery — to his parents, Bill and Jackie Walker, of Suitland, Md.

Dear Mom and Dad,   January 24

Everything is going well, considering. We have moved to our forward assembly area, about 15 miles out of Iraq. I have not personally seen any fighting yet, but I can hear the bombing and small skirmishes in the distance.

I am more confident than ever that we will win this thing and come home. We are overcautious, which is good. Morale is up in my unit and we all want things to begin. . . .

The next time you send a package, please include: pop-top meals (beans and weenies, lasagna), Wet Ones, Pop Tarts, thin (angel hair) spaghetti, olive oil, cloves, garlic salt, summer sausage, tomato sauce, vitamins . . . Take care, I'll write when I can.

Love, Kevin

(Bill Walker, father of Capt. Kevin Walker, said he and his wife have gotten about ten letters from Kevin, a West Point graduate who eventually wants to go into politics. The Walkers sent packages filled with chocolate and strawberry-frosted Pop Tarts, Oreo cookies, potato chips, weenies in a can, towelettes, baby powder, a diary and a sweat suit. They mailed him Christmas decorations and a miniature tree for the holidays, and several funny cards for his birthday Feb. 26.)

■

Brent Boyer, 25, is an infantry scout with the Army's 82nd Airborne Division. In January, Brent's grandmother, Margaret Helen Johnson, died. The following letter was the first he wrote after he had gotten the news.

Dear Mom and Dad,   February 11

Like I told Dad, I love to receive mail, but this wasn't what I intended. I'm sorry Grandma passed away. I'm glad that you were there. I hope she didn't suffer, Mom.

By the time you receive this, I may be part of this big picture over here. I was [with] the Qatari Army. [The Iraqis] went to surrender and when the Qataris went to receive them, the Iraqis opened fire. You won't read or hear this on TV, though. Mom, he's ruthless, and we will be also. We have to fight this madman. . . .

Saddam has said he will wipe out the entire 82nd. Tell him to bring it on. Otherwise I'm fine. Waiting is what is the hardest. I have faith in our President, Dick Cheney, Gen. Colin Powell and Gen. Schwarzkopf in making the right decisions. You are in my thoughts and prayers. I'm sorry Grandma's dead, but she's in a better place now.

Brent

■

Sean Walters, 25, a private with the Army's 101st Airborne Division — to his parents, Ric and Betty Walters, of Osseo, Minn.

Dear Mom and Dad,   February 12

I'm sleeping in my sleeping bag on the ground next to my vehicle. Sgt. "K" is on the hood and the lieutenant is inside. At 0300 hours (3 a.m.) the two platoon guards wake us up. Off in the distance on the horizon looking through our night optical devices we see the bombing and the ADA (air defense artillery). Wow!

Up until about two weeks ago we were on the outskirts of a city. In fact we took over an abandoned house and used it for a command post. It had a TV in it, so for the first week of the war, I, too, watched it on CNN. We can't see the Scuds or the Patriots like you. About all we see are jets and bombers flying overhead and of course a lot of whop-whops [helicopters].

I love you, Sean

9th Marine Regiment Cpl. Carl (Randy) Davis, 30, of Minden, La. — to his sister, Rhonda Graham, of Crestwood, Ky.

Dear Rhonda,   February 17

I love hearing that the flag-making companies are selling out all of their stock. What bothers us here is that we've been getting word that anti-war demonstrators were active in the U.S.A. As the date for the ground offensive draws near, we know all of us won't come home but most of us will, and we look forward to see our friends and families. To everyone in support groups and waving a flag, thank you.

Love y'all, Randy

CHAPTER 3
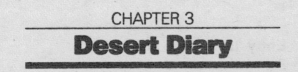
Desert Diary

USA TODAY reporter Laurence Jolidon was one of the first journalists to arrive in Saudi Arabia after President Bush ordered troops to the Persian Gulf. Jolidon found soldiers who had expected to come under fire the minute they got off the plane, but instead were in for months of hard, hot duty in the desert.

For the next five months, Jolidon, an Army veteran of Vietnam, covered the buildup of troops and the anticipation of war. At Christmas, he was still in the gulf, receiving care packages from home and recording the loneliness of soldiers aboard the U.S. Navy hospital ship Mercy.

As the United Nations' Jan. 15 deadline neared, Jolidon was assigned as a pool reporter with the Army's 27th Engineer Battalion (Combat Airborne). The battalion was a unit of about 700 officers and enlisted soldiers responsible for building and fighting — scraping roads out of the desert, breaching minefields and enhancing the mobility of troops around them.

The day before Operation Desert Storm began, Jolidon moved into a dusty tent he shared with engineers. His days were like those of the soldiers — spending time in foxholes, eating Army rations and having trouble sleeping because the allied bombing campaign shattered the night.

Jolidon's Desert Storm diaries differ from much of the

reporting on the gulf war. His are not the stories of smart bombs, high-tech weaponry or sterile views of this "video-game war." Jolidon writes of soldiers sleeping in cold puddles, the good-luck charms they carry, the card games they play. His are stories of the human side of war, the everyday soldiers coping with inconvenience and danger.

Entry 1: Foxhole duty
Published January 25

NEAR THE SAUDI-IRAQI BORDER — In the middle of the night, in every shallow foxhole scratched out of the hard Saudi desert, there's a U.S. soldier waiting for somebody who doesn't know the password.

Between 3:30 a.m. and 6:30 a.m. every day for the past week, one of those soldiers has been Pfc. Kenneth Johns, 24, of Chico, Calif.

"I pray every night," says Johns, "and I hope the Lord is listening. I ask Him to send all the troops home safe and to send a sign to their families back home that everyone over here is safe and will be home soon."

Once in a while, he looks out at the black night, into the mist that makes anything beyond 25 feet invisible, and he thinks about his next birthday, May 2.

He'll be 25. He expects to celebrate it.

"I'm too young to die," he says. "If it's my time, there's nothing I can do about it. But it's not my time. I know it. I've got too many things to go back to, and too much love." And he's single. "That's another reason to get out of here. Get married and have kids."

Talking about his four months here, since arriving Sept. 21, his words rock back and forth between confidence and fear, pride in taking on this dangerous work and the desire to get on with his life beyond this desert.

"This is one big cat box," he says. "Nothing more, nothing less. It's like when you move into a new neighborhood, and there's a bully on the block. Iraq's the bully. We've got to knock him back."

The young trooper sets his jaw firm.

"I'll stay over here as long as I have to. I don't want to come back to this place. We have to do it right this time."

He slips into his reasons for joining the Army.

"Good money, good solid job." Then he adds, "Boy, was I a fool."

But he catches himself. "I'm glad I'm doing it. Glad I'm helping people."

His job for now, though, is to stop people. "I don't like it out here. They can come from any direction. You can hear the jets up there.

"Hopefully, they're ours. I just want to get home safe and sound. I've served my country."

In the middle of the night, hunkered down in the foxhole, he peers into the black and prays, and thinks.

"I talked to my mother an hour before we came up here," he says. "She told me to keep my weapon beside me and my mask on my side. I told her, 'Don't worry, Mom. That's exactly what I'm doing.' "

Entry 2: Life with U.S. troops
Published February 1

WITH U.S. FORCES — The dusty, green tent I'm living in is about the temperature of the vegetable bin in your refrigerator. Well, maybe a little colder.

I can see my breath in the glow of two bare light bulbs hanging from each of the rafter poles. I'm wearing long-johns, shirt and jeans, leather jacket, a British camouflage cotton cap. I'm inhaling coffee and chocolate candy.

It's 9 p.m. here in northeastern Saudi Arabia. The temperature's 38 degrees Fahrenheit and dropping, with a stiff breeze for added chill. There's one floor heater for an entire tent and it's at the end of my cot, but I can't feel any heat. I'd give $100 for the heat stroke I nearly had last August.

I'm sharing the tent with 10 soldiers — men and women, officers and enlisted. They usually live in separate tents. But this is an advance part of a headquarters company. The few tents squeezed into our transport vehicles must be shared until the company brings more.

I'm fortunate. I wear much of the gear and equipment the soldiers do, but I don't carry a weapon or take orders. That confuses some soldiers.

The two most common questions I'm asked: Did my paper order me to cover this story? And do I get paid extra for covering a war? When I say no, they sound genuinely amazed. "Wow, man, then I'd be outta here," one will say.

Strictly combat units are all-male. This headquarters company is about 10 percent female and could be involved in combat. The women are ready to fight. They carry M-16 assault rifles and wear flak jackets.

The women are anxious to be accepted as equals, except that most readily admit they're not as strong as men. Instead of one carrying a big plywood plank for a tent floor, two will carry it. "Not a problem," as soldiers say.

The women prefer mixed tents to all-female tents. "A tent full of women is disgusting," one says. "They all want to be in charge, and they're sloppier."

The sun goes down about 5:30 p.m., but work doesn't stop. Tactical briefings are held. Soldiers must maintain 24-hour communications.

We've been spending a lot of time in bulky clothes that are supposed to protect us from chemical agents that can spew out of Iraqi warheads. Troops call them MOPP suits, for Mission Oriented Protective Posture.

When a chemical alert is sounded, we put on the suits in stages — from MOPP 1 to MOPP 4 — depending on how serious the attack. MOPP 4 is everything: mask, gloves, coat, trousers and big rubber overshoes that look like strips of car tires laced over our boots.

The chemical alerts were so constant that for three days we were under standing order to wear every item except our masks from 6 p.m. to 7 a.m. — considered the most likely time for an Iraqi chemical missile attack.

MOPP suits are warm, so few complained about having to wear them during the day. Night was worse. It's hard to fit comfortably inside a sleeping bag wearing MOPP 3 or 4.

When we moved to this site, the war was already under way. Allied air squadrons were pounding Iraq and Kuwait day and night. Patriot missiles were blowing Scud missiles out of the sky. Navy warships were firing missiles inland.

The Army and Marines were positioning for battle. And we were taking little white pills three times a day. The pills are supposed to increase the effectiveness of the injections we'll give ourselves if we're hit by nerve gas. We also have three sets of anti-nerve-agent serum.

As more people arrived, the camp grew. Tents went up, and gear, supplies and rations went inside.

In a few days, computers were operating in the intelligence and operations tents. A TV set and VCR showed movies every evening in the legal officer's tent.

The count of latrines went from one to three and there was a continuous supply of hot water and a field shower. For the first time in five days I washed my hair. For the first time in months I watched a movie — *Naked Gun*. I stayed up until past midnight writing letters.

We have plenty of food. At all three meals, the cooks put out a box of fresh apples, pears and oranges. Everything else comes in a sealed container.

Breakfast usually is cornflakes, bread (thick slices packed in plastic), peanut butter, jelly, milk, sugared fruit drinks, sodas, coffee, M&Ms and, once, Twinkies.

For lunch and dinner there's a choice:

MREs — meals ready to eat — individually packaged, super starchy and served cold or heated.

MOREs — microwaved, ready to eat — mostly gravy with small portions of beef, chicken or spaghetti.

The talk of enlisted soldiers — among themselves and inside a mixed tent — is quick, lively and coarse, like you would hear around a shopping mall or a college dorm.

Everyone shares — candy, gripes, information, letters, music and living space.

Most important, we share the knowledge that we're soon headed for a battle zone and we could be together longer — or more briefly — than we'd like to be.

Entry 3: Where saluting stops
Published February 5

WITH U.S. FORCES — Military life can be harder than it has to be.

One Army unit commander declared his camp a no-saluting area soon after moving to a site near the Iraqi border. In wartime, officers prefer not to be saluted while in range of enemy soldiers who might want to eliminate them so lower-ranking troops won't have anyone to give them any orders.

A week or so later, the commander switched back to a must-salute policy. Soldiers visiting from a nearby unit were caught off guard. When they failed to offer the proper salute, they got either a cold shoulder or a reprimand.

The Army combat engineers I've been with don't salute in their camp. We're either very close or incredibly close to the Iraqi border, depending on whether you consult an old map or a new one.

Newer maps show a more northern boundary — by a few "clicks," or kilometers. Saddam Hussein must have given up some of this barren ground after 1984, when the map I have was published.

The weather has begun to warm in our part of this vast desert. It's raining and as windy as Chicago. A week ago there were white crystals of morning frost on the tents and people found excuses to do things inside.

This is such a strange and forsaken part of the world to them, the soldiers try to draw parallels to places they know or to places were they would like to be.

The engineers' new camp "looks a lot like the National Weapons Firing Center around Yakima to me," says Capt. Steve Janzen, 29, of Moscow, Idaho. Janzen commands a platoon of Army reserve firefighters based in Washington state and currently attached to the 27th Engineers. The view here can't match the one at home. "Back there, I look out and there's Moscow Mountain."

Here he sees a flat pan of land so infertile and lifeless lizards won't live on it.

The first morning I went to breakfast in Bravo Company's mess hall with my public affairs escort — Spec. Kimberly Godon, 27, of North Carolina, the only woman in this camp right now — was an event.

Hulking men weighted down with armored vests, parkas, web belts, canteens, ammo and rifles looked up from plates of eggs and potatoes covered with ground-beef gravy and gaped at her.

Godon is a reservist called to active duty to help the Army handle the U.S. media pool covering the war. Back home in North Carolina, she lives in a converted tobacco barn, taking college courses and caring for a small farm full of horses, dogs, goats and pigs. She carries photos of her four-legged "family" around with her, proudly showing them.

She also carries a .45-caliber pistol, two bayonets and camera gear for taking pictures to go with the stories she writes about this war for official Army publications.

There's one other woman at the camp now, a clerk who was deployed to Saudi Arabia with the firefighters — Spec. Donna Brown, 32, of San Francisco. She's just returned from a rear-area unit after being ordered back when commanders thought she would be too close to combat if she stayed with her platoon. She fought the transfer, arguing her job was "interchangeable" — open to either a male or female soldier.

"It's pretty scary up here," she says. "I don't sleep well." But she would rather be with combat soldiers, she says, because they know their way around a war zone.

Last Sunday was a rare day off for the 27th Engineers, the first in about a month. Meal hours were "adjusted" so the troops could sleep in.

There was no mandatory training. The soldiers were allowed to rest, relax, do laundry, write letters, watch a movie in the mess hall.

They're hoping some new tapes will arrive. Twice in the past few days they've seen *Over the Top* with Sylvester Stallone. The battalion chaplain visited the company areas for chapel services. Lately, more soldiers have been staying afterward for a few personal words with him.

After the sun goes down, the sounds of planes and helicopters flying north to hit targets in Iraq begin. Every night we can hear bombs exploding in the distance.

There's a war up there, but we're not in it yet.

Entry 4: Drills keep troops on toes
Published February 11

WITH U.S. FORCES — New foxholes showed up in the campground this week, dug by and for combat engineers just moving up from the rear. Each foxhole is fortified with sandbags on three sides. Today's military calls these shallow cuts in the earth "fighting positions," but that's just a glorified name for what older soldiers called foxholes.

Every soldier in this unit — plus a reporter — must don a battle uniform and remain stationed, soldiers with weapons, in their assigned hole for 30 minutes every morning and another 30 minutes every evening for what's called a "stand-to."

At a stand-to, the camp is in a defensive position to repel an enemy attack. The twice-daily drills have generated some griping, but most of the soldiers don't question them. "If the Iraqis come, we're ready for them," says Spec. Robert Hoobler, 23, of Warren, Pa., a construction surveyor.

Another surveyor, Spec. Joe Kingston, 20, of Detroit, says the drills have a function. "It's like a little practice," he says. "We need to know where to go and what to do if something does happen, so it'll be routine."

And huddling in the dirt against the morning chill, there's some bonding to be done. "If we have any stress or any problems, we work things out among ourselves."

Sitting in their fighting positions, the combat engineers can't play cards, listen to music or write letters, as they like to do when they have free time. But they can talk.

Spec. Charles Allen, 23, of Bozeman, Mont., was going to re-enlist when his time was up next August, "but then this came along." He's thinking about going to school to become a dental technician. "After three years in the dirt, I can stand being in a building drilling on people."

Hoobler was due for a break Jan. 23 on the luxury liner *Cunard Princess* — rented by the Pentagon and anchored off Bahrain. But the war started.

"One of my sergeants had offered me $100 for it, too, and I turned him down," Hoobler says. "I guess I should have sold it. But he probably would have demanded his money back anyway."

The engineers say they're more nervous now than before Jan. 16. "If somebody touches me when I'm asleep," says Kingston, "I'll jump. I never used to do that."

And they're tired of filling sandbags. "I'll bet we've filled 20,000 sandbags, just our section, since we got here last fall," says Hoobler. He says he's filled 9,000 himself.

After five more minutes, the "stand-to" is over and everyone disperses. Some go back to bed. Some go to work. Some go to breakfast.

Breakfast is becoming a slapdash affair. One morning, the only hot food was eggs and salty vegetable-rice soup.

The one box of instant oatmeal was empty. The fresh-fruit carton offered only small, bruised apples. There were boxes of cornflakes, but no milk, only sugared pineapple drink, to pour on them. Some soldiers opted for peanut-butter-and-jelly sandwiches and coffee.

Newly arrived troops brought a welcome surprise: a small microwave oven. Strictly a rear-area appliance, the microwave is excellent for heating MREs or canned goods from home. The microwave doesn't look out of place in today's U.S. military, which takes its computers, faxes and copying machines to the field. But the machines take a beating in this climate.

A few days ago, an officer and sergeant from one engineer unit went to a nearby town to buy more durable equipment: eight portable, manual typewriters.

Reporters who brought laptop computers and mini-printers are switching to klutzy old manual typewriters, the kind they make in Third World countries now. They even work in a foxhole.

Entry 5: Poetry and war
Published February 12

WITH U.S. FORCES — Valentine's Day is approaching, and Capt. Michelle Perna is stationed in Saudi Arabia, far from those she loves. Her husband, George Albertini, Jr., waits for her back in Washington, D.C., praying for her safety and writing love poems to her.

The poems "really help me get through all of this," says Perna, an Army transport officer with the 507th Support Group near the Kuwait border.

For Albertini, the verses he lovingly composes help ease the pain of their separation. "Of course, I wish she were back here, safe," says Albertini, who met Perna when he was a police lieutenant in Greenville, N.C., lecturing in one of her college classes. "But Michelle's very dedicated. She's very, very patriotic. One of her favorite scenes is the Statue of Liberty — that's her lady."

Albertini says his wife is in the Army "because she really believes in what she's doing. I knew from the beginning, when this all started, that she would want to go and be a part of it."

Before the Iraqi invasion of Kuwait, Perna, 24, had planned to shift from regular Army to reserve. Albertini, her husband of three years, had moved to Washington to work at her father's construction company. Before she joined her husband in the capital, however, she wanted her promotion to captain.

When her captain's bars came through last summer, she filed her resignation papers. Then what she calls "the Kuwait thing" blew up Aug. 2.

"The only hesitation I have," says Albertini, "is I don't believe they [women] are getting enough credit for the work they do. As far as being able to do the job, I have no hesitation at all. My wife can outperform a lot of her male peers."

Until she returns, Perna will have to cling to Albertini's love verses. "He used to write poems when we first met," says Perna, "but he hadn't for a while. Now he's writing them again."

A selection of George Albertini's poetry, written for his Army wife, Capt. Michelle Perna:

Storm clouds are on the horizon
Watch for the moonless night
Gather together your words of death
And meet on the desert to fight.

The pace has quickened, adrenaline flows,
Now ready yourself for war
The eyes of the world are upon you
As destiny knocks at your door.

All that is right stands with you
In the test that is yet to come.
Remember we love you when days turn dark
And your spirit grows weary and numb.

We stand humbled by your sacrifice
As you enter the dark side of the sun.
Your purpose gives hope to all free people,
Your cause is a noble one.

So remember my love in the coming days
As you face this cold cruel test
Through the screaming hell of shot and shell
You are our country's best.

Entry 6: Life in Hanerville
Published February 18

WITH U.S. TROOPS IN SAUDI ARABIA — The tall, wood-frame sign over the entrance to this military truck stop reads "Welcome to Hanerville." Don't bother looking it up in your Rand McNally.

Hanerville is only about six weeks old. It's located on a big highway, between somewhere in Saudi Arabia and a lot of other somewheres. It's open 24 hours, every day.

The sign was painted by Army Staff Sgt. Mitch Haner, 34, of North Tonawanda, N.Y. Thus the name.

"I told him if he painted all the signs, I'd name it after him," says Capt. Scott Verbeuge, 30, of Salt Lake City, who calls himself "the mayor of Hanerville."

Already, Hanerville has an outstanding reputation among the military truck drivers and shotgun riders who are piling up a record number of miles in this long, logistics-mad operation. One captain gave it five stars.

Verbeuge and Lt. John Gaudino, 26, of Wells, Maine, compare Hanerville to "Little America," a famous, sprawling truck stop outside Cheyenne, Wyo.

Hanerville has tents for a permanent party and many more for transients. The mess hall offers choice Army meals, like veal cutlet and creamed corn, complete with lemon cake and occasional cherry cobblers. For those with a junk-food appetite, there's the Wolfburgermobile, a hamburger joint on wheels that serves hamburgers made of some kind of red meat, hot dogs made of some kind of sausage and french fries. The lines are long but the service is friendly.

Gaudino, Hanerville's "deputy mayor," is a banker back home. But he also is a member of the Army reserves, and his unit was activated for the war.

There's not much need for a banker's skills at Hanerville. Everything's free if you're a military person, or escorted by one, and anyone who's not welcome. So Gaudino helps Verbeuge keep order around the camp and helps with the media tour.

Haner still drops by occasionally. He was here the other day to pick up wood to make signs for a similar place. He doesn't expect it to be named Hanerville, though. "One's enough," he says. "This was my first big project."

A lot of Army camp life is a tradeoff. Rain ponchos for boots. Polypropylene underwear for webbed belts. Parkas and padded liners for a bayonet. An extra pair of desert "cammies" for cigarettes, fried chicken or a portable tent heater.

Although soldiers know the military bureaucracy is supposed to equip and supply them, they also know the system can deny them things they require.

So they help each other get what they need. They hook each other up. Around the official supply fringes of every Army camp is a bazaar.

Some U.S. soldiers who've gotten bored with eating their own government's packaged rations — meals, ready to eat — started scoring some of the French army rations.

The French food comes in a cardboard, shoebox-size carton that contains enough for a single soldier for one day and includes tins of sardines and tuna, thicker crackers than the U.S. variety, and better entrees.

The Americans really liked the French MREs. The French could barely tolerate the U.S. MREs. Most of those deals are on the back burner now.

Entry 7: Night in an Army camp
Published February 21

WITH U.S. FORCES IN SAUDI ARABIA — Action doesn't quit when the sun sets over the desert at an Army combat unit camp.

The intensified allied bombing campaign lights up the sky to the north. Flashes — like lightning — radiate for a second, then disappear. A silver crescent moon makes the void behind it that much blacker.

Soldiers on guard duty or driving between camps watch the flashes and try to estimate distance by counting the seconds until they feel a tremor or hear a rumble from the explosions.

Monday after midnight, the rumbling came at regular intervals for nearly an hour. The results at ground level — craters, chaos, flames, death, despair — are left to the imagination.

"I hope we get to see what's happening up there," says Pfc. Denao Ruttino, 19, of San Diego. "This waiting is terrible."

Ruttino joined the Army two years ago, with his parents' permission. He has spent much of that time in the field as an airborne engineer — in Arkansas, Honduras and now here.

For good luck, he carries a small Bible that contains an Italian swimming medal won by his father in the late 1940s. Victor Ruttino "was the best swimmer in Trieste," his son says. "He was supposed to go to the Olympics, but he broke his arm."

As he talks, Ruttino wraps black coils of detonator cord around narrow bricks of explosives and canisters of TNT about the size of a can of shaving cream.

Ruttino is a "sapper," schooled in the ways of laying

and disarming demolition charges. He is accumulating knowledge and skills that would take much longer under normal training schedules.

When the sun goes down, the camp becomes a haunted-looking place of shadows and forms. Laundry hanging on ropes outside and sheets of camouflage netting make tents look like steep burial mounds. The concertina wire around some tents can't be seen — it has to be memorized, unless you don't mind sharp barbs in your hands or legs.

A few soldiers lounge in the mess tent, drinking coffee, watching tapes on the VCR — music videos, movies or the 1991 Super Bowl with its patriotic halftime show. Clips from the first days of the air war always draw shouts and hoo-hahs.

Inside the tents, they pass around photos from women they've written to over the past few months. Some are girlfriends they knew when they shipped out. Even more are females they've never met.

For card players, there's usually a game of spades around a big pot of coffee and a small pot of cash.

Sgt. 1st Class Mike Panaranto, 36, of Terre Haute, Ind., and 1st Sgt. Freddy Ferreyra, 41, of New York City, are the big spade wielders of B Company, 27th Engineer Battalion. Their reputations are fierce.

"We don't cheat," says Ferreyra, "but we play by our own rules," which include a few versions newcomers have never seen before.

In the Tactical Operations Center, the company's 24-hour radio and briefing room, the lights never go out. Spec. Allen Rogers, 22, of Kent, Ohio, and Spec. Roger Hollins, 23, of Arkansas City, Kan., split the duty on the TOC switchboard.

Soldiers drift into the TOC at night to pick up and drop off mail.

More mail is going out than coming in these days, and the unit feels more isolated the longer the waiting goes on. The Army post office system changed the battalion's overseas mailing address when it moved north last month, and no letters with the new address have reached them.

Ferreyra stops in after a card game to catch up on messages from other units and to answer some letters. "The last one I got was a Christmas card," he says.

A brash-sounding taskmaster with a black-bristle mustache, he has spent most of his two decades in the Army in the field and overseas.

But his drill-instructor voice still bears the stamp of the Big Apple, where his two brothers are police officers.

"They're having a big argument back there," he says, "because they're putting yellow ribbons on the precinct stations and flag patches on their uniforms. The city says that's a no-no. But they want to support the troops. I think they should."

By 10:30, most of the soldiers are asleep. Nights are warmer than a few weeks ago, but still cold enough to require heaters and sleeping bags.

Army-issue bags aren't warm enough for some soldiers, so they add body bags, the green plastic bags for sending home Americans killed in action. When a soldier mentions he's sleeping in a body bag, others in his tent usually say they don't want to tempt fate.

"You're not going to catch me in a body bag," one soldier says. "I don't want to go home in one, so they don't need to size me for it."

Entry 8: A tragic "ride up the road"
Published March 4

*After his Feb. 20 communication with USA TODAY,
Jolidon traveled with the combat engineers in northeastern Saudi Arabia and into Iraq as the ground offensive
was launched. USA TODAY editors at the time didn't
know of his position or safety because his pool reports
weren't reaching the States. The following entry was filed
after Jolidon returned to Dhahran, Saudi Arabia, on
March 3.*

IN U.S.-OCCUPIED IRAQ — U.S. Army combat engineers, part of the assault along the western flank of
Iraq's bomb-shattered defenses, had an easy time reaching their first objective — a major Iraqi air base at As
Salman.

Instead of minefields and tank ditches on the road
north, the 27th Engineer Battalion encountered light resistance and thousands of Iraqi troops eager to surrender.

The battalion's mission was to turn the base into a
supply hub, then move east. Enemy divisions collapsed
so quickly across southern Iraq, the base was never needed for moving supplies.

Only one flight left the airfield. On Day Three of the
ground war, a helicopter lifted off with the bodies of sev-
en engineers who, while clearing mines, accidentally triggered a cluster bomb dropped earlier by a U.S. aircraft.

All the dead, along with one wounded, were from Alpha Co. By dusk, Alpha's vehicle antennas flew U.S. flags
at half-staff. "Their platoon is devastated," said Spec.
Daniel Bartz, 21, of Sheboygan, Wis. "Best friends are
gone, your dad is gone, your buddy, your brother."

The deaths came while the engineers were impatiently

wondering if the war would ever be a test of their months of desert training. Staff Sgt. Lynn Smith, 26, of Oklahoma City, a squad leader in Bravo Company of the 27th, probably said it best for thousands of soldiers in The Hundred Hours War.

"We basically rode up this road," he said, "with magazines in our weapons, without firing a shot. We just sat through the whole war on this road."

The day before the ground war started was the six-month anniversary of the 27th Battalion's arrival in the Persian Gulf. The soldiers are still far from home, but when it's time to leave, the roads they've built from one end of this desert to the other will take them there.

Here's a look at the combat engineers' sweep into southeastern Iraq:

SUNDAY, FEB. 24: After a 3 a.m. wake-up, we look north from our assembly area and imagine what awaits us in Iraq. Nothing good, but everyone hopes it will be over soon.

The radio says President Bush has authorized a ground offensive.

Spec. David Shaw, 23, of El Paso, Texas, has the freshest uniforms and newest equipment in his squad. He got here nine days ago from Fort Ord, Calif. "The good thing about being assigned to this unit is they've been here so long. Hopefully, they'll be one of the first sent back."

A lot of guys are packing good-luck charms. Women's panties are popular. "I've carried a pair of women's panties in my helmet for the past 20 years," says Sgt. 1st Class Charles Zehring, 39, of Alexandria, Va. "Not the same pair, of course."

At 5 a.m., word comes to move out. As we cross the border, our convoy is a ghostly row of pin-pricked headlights.

Driving north, the smell of gunpowder hangs under the gray sky. There's no enemy in sight. Rumors swirl that the Iraqis are surrendering.

Some soldiers are disappointed. "By the time that we see action, everybody will be waving a white flag," says Pvt. Clayton Schroeder, 24, of Wausau, Wis.

"I wish some Iraqis would surrender to me," says Pfc. Denao Ruttino, 19, of San Diego, "so I could feel like I was in this war."

The engineers begin coming upon Iraqis waiting beside the road, unarmed and unguarded, looking for someone to take them prisoner.

One group of 45 came walking down the highway directly into the path of the 20th Brigade commander, Col. Robert Flowers, 43, of Kane, Pa. He ordered two squads to confine them behind barbed wire. "Obviously," says Flowers, "they're not fighting to the death."

MONDAY, FEB. 25: The western flank is slower than the rest. With no resistance, the engineers' convoy stops at 6 p.m. Rest time until 7 a.m.

U.S. troops are allowed only light with red filters after dark to avoid giving away their positions. When we woke up at 4 a.m., the French had parked a bus with 30 Iraqi prisoners next to Bravo Company's trucks.

At dawn, 155mm howitzers and multiple-launch rocket systems start up — loud enough to make ear drums hurt. "Good morning, Iraq!" Schroeder shouts.

The day is slow. At noon, engineers are ordered to set fire to an abandoned Iraqi truck. The soldiers are excited by the action.

At nightfall, the convoy is still a little short of the airfield at As Salman. The radio carries news about Marines closing in on Kuwait City.

"That's the end of this field problem," says Sean Nesbit, 20, of Charlotte, N.C.

TUESDAY, FEB. 26: The engineers move on As Salman, hit by bombs that left only a few craters in the runways. Unexploded bombs lie everywhere. All morning, strong winds whip across the base, sending up a blinding sandstorm. Soldiers huddle in their vehicles.

Every hour or so, a loud explosion shakes the field from soldiers setting off the undetonated bombs. One explosion quickly follows another. The broken sequence catches all ears. Just ahead of where we are sitting, seven engineers lay dead.

The accident angers and puzzles other engineers. "You can go to school after school and learn about these things," says Sgt. Mike Panaranto, 36, of Terre Haute, Ind., "and they'll teach you exactly how each explosive is supposed to act and react. Then you go out and try it and it'll do something different. You have to really respect this stuff."

WEDNESDAY, FEB. 27: The 27th Engineers leave the air base at dawn.

"Our orders are to stay on the road and wait for new grid coordinates," says commander Lt. Col. Ron Stewart, 43, of Williamsburg, Va. "In other words, keep moving until we tell you to stop."

The battalion is told not to build supply bases, as originally planned. But the engineers keep scraping roads out of the crusty sand until they link up with other forces.

Mechanics work under a bright full moon repairing brakes and fixing flat tires. The long deployment has taken a toll on their aging vehicles.

"They gave us new engines after we got over here," says Sgt. Paul Sullivan, a squad leader from Irondequoit, N.Y. "We kept them running."

This is Sullivan's thirtieth birthday. He breaks out a tin of blueberry cake and a pan of chocolate pudding, both military rations. "I've had these stored for the past five months, just waiting for this occasion," he says.

THURSDAY, FEB. 28: The cease-fire began today. The engineers are relieved. "We had overwhelming superiority," says Sgt. Maj. Richard Knox of Chattanooga, Tenn. "Around the world, other armies are overrated and the U.S. Army is underrated."

The engineers proceed to push north and east toward the Euphrates River, then halt to await the outcome of U.S.-Iraqi surrender talks.

The soldiers are idle. Their task is to help clear some of the 500,000 mines the Iraqis are said to have spread across the desert of southern Iraq and Kuwait.

As they learned from As Salman airfield, mines are deadly even after the war is over.

In the following week, as Iraq and the U.S. met on peace terms, Jolidon remained in the gulf, recording the stories of soldiers as they trudged in from the field. Plans called for him to wrap up his reporting quickly, return to the United States and take a long vacation.

CHAPTER 4

Volunteers and Victors

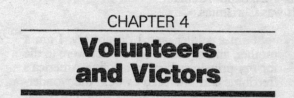

Inside tanks in the desert, in the air over Baghdad, in the waters of the Persian Gulf, U.S. troops faced the enemy with bravery.

For most, it was their first taste of war and the fear that comes with it. For many, the long days of waiting were almost as bad as the quick pace of battle.

These stories are about typical soldiers and the jobs they did: the doctor, fighter pilot, minefield expert, priest, woman commander. Here are parents, sons, daughters, husbands and wives. The Americans, and what they did.

A soldier and a mother

The day before her son, Jonathan, turned 6, Army Spec. Alyssa Mehl kissed him good- bye — and went to war.

No one knows how many mothers were among the women soldiers serving in the Persian Gulf.

But the image of fatigue-clad women kissing their children goodbye unsettled a nation more accustomed to sending its men off to war.

In a series of touching letters home to her husband and three sons, Alyssa Mehl, 27, of Fort Eustis, Va., told of her loneliness — and her pride. She wrote from her post with the 119th Transportation Company in King Abdul Aziz Port, Saudi Arabia.

It was Christmas.

"I am a soldier, and I do not cry. I am a mother, and my heart breaks. If I were to die for my principles here, protecting America's freedoms and interests, I would die wondering, 'What have I taught my children? What have I taken from them?'"

Back home, Jonathan drew pictures of tears and fire. Philip, 4, spun a globe in search of mom. And Thomas, 2, was too young to understand.

Husband Tom Mehl is the boys' stepfather. He married Alyssa only months earlier. He quit his $20,000-a-year auto mechanic's job to play, in his words, "Susie Homemaker." He took care of the kids. "There is no such thing as a 'Mr. Mom,'" he said. "There's a love from a mom that a dad can't give. Moms are the soft things. They're the ones who take care of the bruises and scrapes. There's something I'm lacking. I try to be both but I can't. There's no way."

Until regulations were loosened in 1975, most pregnant women or those with dependent children were barred from active military duty. The gulf war is the first major deployment in which large numbers of mothers are serving. "It is unprecedented for [this] many mothers to be over there," said military historian Bettie Morden.

Son Philip thinks he understands why his mom was overseas. "My mommy is over there because she needs to fight someone," he said. "A man is taking away people's houses."

"Someday they might have to make war," said Jonathan. "When they fight, they die."

"God makes them come back alive," said Philip.

"No," his brother said. "They will never come back."

Their mother wrote of her sadness at being away, and the jealousy she felt for women who were safe at home with their children. Still, she was proud:

> "I envy you, who sit reading this at home.
> Yes, I made my choice — and I would
> again — to become a member of the U.S.
> Army. Still, I envy you the freedoms I am
> protecting. I am a soldier. I am well trained,
> confident, honorable, brave.
>
> I am part of Operation Desert Shield. My
> country calls me a hero. I do not cry."

The head of logistics

The U.S. Army spent $80 million a month on supplies for Operation Desert Storm — and the head of logistics, Army Lt. Gen. William "Gus" Pagonis, kept track of them.

Falling back on the training he got working at his parents' restaurant, U.S. Army Lt. Gen. William "Gus" Pagonis successfully pulled off the largest logistical move in recent history: supplying Operation Desert Storm.

Under his supervision, everything from beans to bullets made their way to the bleak Middle Eastern desert.

"Pagonis started out with a handful of sand and built a logistical structure over there that's kind of amazing," said Maj. Gen. Charles Murray of the Army Materiel Command.

Pagonis, 49, did it with a sense of humor, too.

He set up "Wolfburger" stands, where U.S. soldiers could get hamburgers, french fries and hot dogs. He opened "Tiffany's" — a mobile field kitchen that served pancakes and heaps of hot scrambled eggs at a desert air base. To give bored soldiers a little R&R, Pagonis turned an Aramco oil barge into a "floating hotel" off the Saudi Arabia coast with air conditioning and hot showers. He also opened a base camp "recreation center," where 600 troops a day could watch movies, swim or play basketball and volleyball.

"It'll be a great one-stop thing," Pagonis said at the time, "a great fun day for a kid to get out of the desert, relax, listen to American-type music, read books, write letters." Or, he added, "Just sleep all day."

Pagonis' efforts won him a third general's star from Gen. Norman Schwarzkopf.

Pagonis learned how to "take care of people" working in his family's restaurant, and in an all-night restaurant in Charleroi, Pa., where he dished out spaghetti, hamburgers and other short-order fare. In fact, he says he's kept the U.S. Central Command's expenses down by 50 percent by using the tough tactics of negotiating and competitive bidding that he learned as a kid.

His love for the military came later as an ROTC student at Penn State. "He liked it from the very beginning," said his aunt Mary Pagonis. "He told me he didn't care for Pentagon desk jobs — he wanted the field."

The first in his family to join the military, Pagonis is also a student of history. His favorite topic: How German Gen. Erwin Rommel's Afrika Korps won desert battles in World War II — but lost the campaign because of its inability to keep supplies moving to the front.

"The [British] defeated Rommel by building bases forward as they went and not having to go back for supplies," he said. It's a plan that worked as well for the Americans in the gulf war as it did for the British in World War II.

A battlefield priest

Lt. Col. Vincent Inghilterra had to adapt to the religious restrictions of Muslim Saudi Arabia to minister to some of the 175,000 U.S. Catholic troops.

At first glance, Army Lt. Col. Vincent Inghilterra looked like any other officer — the desert camouflage uniform, the insignia, the helmet.

Yet he carried no weapon. Inside his pocket was a tiny prayer book. In the pouch where soldiers carried ammunition were a dozen rosaries.

Inghilterra, 48, is a Catholic priest who was in charge of deploying 114 Catholic chaplains to Operation Desert Storm. It was too few, he said, for the 175,000 Catholic troops there.

A former parish priest in Paterson, N.J., Inghilterra was on active duty for seven years and served as a chaplain in Turkey and Germany for five years, before he went to the gulf in August. "There's no other place I'd want to be," he said. "This is where I am needed, even though it's difficult."

The Saudi ban on religions other than Islam — and the push by the U.S. military to discourage public shows of religion among U.S. troops — made Inghilterra's job tough. He adapted. At a dedication for a dining hall financed by Saudi Arabia on a huge air base, he used an ecumenical prayer. "Oh God, Allah," he began. He ended: "May the God of all of us bless us all."

Ministers of all faiths were asked to conceal the cross they wore when among Saudi civilians. At many units, announcements of worship services were made in a kind of code. Services were called "morale meetings." Denominations were "P meetings" for Protestants, "C meetings" for Catholics, and "J meetings" for Jews.

Despite the restrictions, Inghilterra went about the sometimes grim duty of a battlefield chaplain. He said the final prayers over the bodies of Catholic Marines slain in fighting near the Kuwait border. And he remained emphatic about his duty, saying before the ground war began, "For every Catholic that leaves this [war] theater in a body bag, the families will know that a priest has done the prayer of commendation."

An F-15 pilot

In the initial hours of the first night of war, Air Force captain and F-15 pilot Steve Tate made the first kill of Operation Desert Storm.

At 20,000 feet, two hours and 10 minutes after take-off, Capt. Steve Tate watched in awe as F-117A Stealth bombers let loose their laser-guided bombs over Iraq.

The 2,000-pound bombs were precise and deadly. "The entire city was just sparkling at us," he said. For Tate, leader of the squad, the night had just begun.

The husky 28-year-old from Watersmeet, Mich., would soon meet a "bogey" — the nickname for an Iraqi fighter pilot. Tate saw the Iraqi jet off his wing and whipped around to chase him. He put the bogey in his laser sights and ripped off a Sparrow missile. The missile hit the Iraqi jet dead on.

"I could see a piece of the airplane blowing up," Tate said later. "It was a huge fireball. I don't anticipate anyone got out of that."

Five hours later, the pilots arrived back at the air base in central Saudi Arabia to cheering, saluting and thumps on the back.

"I feel good," Tate said. "I've never experienced this before. It's unfortunate we had to go to war, but I guess there is no other way."

Tate's father, Maurice, was on the telephone with a reporter at his home in Michigan, when he saw his son on the television screen. It was the first time he'd laid eyes on him since the pilot was deployed in August. Tate, who enlisted in 1980, is stationed at Langley Air Force Base, Va., where he lives with his wife and two children. "The mustache is new," the elder Tate said, his voice cracking, as he watched the TV screen. "It was a long night."

"We're very proud of that boy," World War II veteran Dale Jenkins said at the Watersmeet township hall. "The town is a-buzzin'."

A civilian minefield expert

Bill Schneck designed a device that helped U.S. troops break through traps set by Iraq.

When Army combat engineers realized they were headed for the world's largest minefield, they asked Bill Schneck to come along. Schneck does mines.

"I'll get you through any minefield if I've got all day — with no casualties," he said confidently. "When you need to get through one quickly, that's when you start paying a price to a minefield."

Iraq is believed to have had one of the world's most

complete inventories of land mines. Thousands were laid in a tiered web of obstacles and barriers stretching for miles along Iraq's borders and inside Kuwait.

"The threat [for U.S. forces] is about as complex as it could have gotten when it comes to mines," Schneck said. Schneck, 30, is a civilian who worked in the Army's research and development center at Fort Belvoir, Va. But the Kansas City, Mo., native has served as an Army officer with the airborne combat engineers. When the engineers were looking for help, they called Schneck.

He rigged a number of innovative devices for clearing mines. One was a kind of grappling hook fitted over the barrel of an M-16 rifle. A 100-meter cord kept the hook tied to the gun. An engineer fired a blank shot from the M-16, and the charge sent the hook flying out the length of the cord. When the hook was pulled in, tripwires from mines laid across its path were triggered. The mines blew up. Some, like the "bouncing Betty," would bounce 25 meters before exploding.

But soldiers were 100 meters away — unharmed.

Staff Sgt. Robert Chute, 29, of Windham, N.H., a squad leader in B Company, 27th Engineer Battalion [Combat Airborne], said the rifle-fired device "has worked every time we've done it. It lands within a meter or two of where it's aimed. It only takes a few minutes, and we plan to use it every step of the way."

Chute knew before the ground war began that the device could be a life-saver.

"We're extremely pleased with it," he said. "It's going to save our ass big-time."

A soldier is alive

Ruth Dillow was at her job when the Army officer arrived. He said her son, Clayton Carpenter, had been killed. A day later, the telephone rang again. It was Clayton — wounded, but alive.

Pfc. Clayton Carpenter came within five feet of death in Iraq. Bad enough. But his parents went through worse — they were told he'd been killed.

Wounded by shrapnel from an explosion that killed two members of his unit, Carpenter arrived March 5 at the 10th Aeromedical Staging Flight at Andrews Air Force Base, Md., a way station for wounded soldiers going home. "I've gotten the VIP treatment because I'm supposed to be dead," Carpenter joked.

Evacuated first to a hospital in Saudi Arabia, Carpenter learned that his parents, back in Kansas, had been notified he was dead. He got on the phone to tell them otherwise. "Mom, I'm alive!" he said. However, persuading his mother, Ruth Dillow of Chanute, Kan., wasn't easy. "When I got hold of her, she didn't believe it was me," Carpenter said. She quizzed him. He had to identify his high school classmates and principal, and tell her about the death of a close friend in a car accident.

"It was such a shock. I was afraid somebody was playing with my mind," Dillow said. Half an hour later, she was convinced. Twenty-four hours of grieving were ended.

"I'll be coming home alive, walking and talking," said Carpenter, although he arrived at Andrews on crutches because of a shrapnel wound in his foot.

Carpenter's own moments of terror came on Feb. 26

when his unit, part of the 1st Cavalry Division of Ft. Hood, Texas, strayed into Iraqi territory. Before turning around, a member of his unit picked up a small, cone-shaped metal "souvenir" that turned out to be a bomblet — or mini-bomb. It exploded.

Carpenter, five feet away, threw up his hands to protect his face, then discovered them covered in blood. "I thought I'd been hit in the face," he said. "I thought I'd been blinded."

He wasn't seriously hurt. But two other soldiers were dead.

"I looked down. They were lying on the ground. They were gone. I didn't know what to do. None of my training came through at the time. I was just in shock." The Army has apologized for its mistake in falsely reporting his death, he said. "They're still trying to find out how it happened."

A soldier's teddy bear

Army 1st Lt. Amy Beth Stuart won a measure of fame while serving in Desert Storm. Not for her bravery, but for her photo. [See photo insert]

A picture of 24-year-old Amy Beth Stuart, a nurse from Germantown, N.Y., landed on front pages of newspapers across the country Feb. 25 after a pool photographer took a shot of her napping — with her teddy bear.

The photo got plenty of reaction. Many thought it showed one of those seldom seen private and quiet moments of war. Some thought it wrongly revived a sexist stereotype of women's roles in the military — namely, the pretty-nurse image.

As transmitted from the front and as published, the photo was accompanied by no more information than the sketchy data supplied by the photographer. All it said was "Nurse Amy Stuart, assigned to the 5th MASH unit, snuggles with a teddy bear as she takes a nap in Saudi Arabia. DOD Pool photo by David Turnley."

It wasn't until after the *Times Union* in Albany published the photo on its front page that its editors found out Lt. Stuart was from the nearby town of Germantown. The *Times Union* followed up with a big feature story.

Elsewhere, the photo was the subject of talk shows. People called newspapers asking how they could write to Stuart. Men wanted to propose.

Meanwhile, it turned out that nurse Stuart only *looked* as soft and vulnerable as the bear she cuddled in the photo. "Hard as nails," said Mark Stuart, one of three brothers she left behind when called to Desert Storm. "She's a nurse first," said Mark, "but definitely a soldier second. When the training calls for rappelling, she goes down the rope head first."

The bear was a gift from Stuart's mother, Doris, one of two she bought her. Wanting to spare her daughter any embarrassment, she asked Amy if it would be okay to ship one to Saudi Arabia.

All who were touched by the photo are glad Stuart gave the okay. And many agree with Mark, who said the photo "shows she's tough enough to be a soldier. And tough enough to be a woman, too."

When 1st Lt. Amy Beth Stuart returns to Germantown, the other teddy bear will be waiting. It should come as no surprise, either, that it is dressed in a uniform — the camouflage of the Army Green Berets.

A Navy surgeon

Navy Cmdr. John Wilckens wanted to learn about combat surgery, but instead learned about himself.

John Wilckens is an orthopedic surgeon who has been in the Navy for 14 years.

When the gulf war began, he braced himself for a flood of casualties — 15 or 20 surgeries a day. But instead he found himself wondering if his skills would get rusty from lack of practice.

U.S. casualties were much lower than anyone expected. Throughout the war, 339 soldiers were wounded.

"As a surgeon, I would have liked to have that surgical experience" of intense combat, he said. "But I am joyfully disappointed that I didn't."

That doesn't mean Wilckens didn't see action. His medical group was the northernmost Navy unit in Saudi Arabia, near the Iraq border. Once the ground war began, so did a stream of wounded soldiers. "There were a couple of times the chopper would come in with 10 or 12 patients, and as you're going to casualty receiving, you have this anxiety," he said. "When you actually lay your eyes on a patient and see the magnitude of his injuries, instincts take over. It could have been my brother laying on the stretcher, and I wouldn't even know it." That kind of pressure took its toll. "You become a machine."

Those battlefield experiences have made him a better doctor, he thinks, because he couldn't rely on machines. "I've matured as a physician and I trust my intuition a lot more," he said.

Wilckens, 36, of Camp Lejeune, N.C., has realized he can operate under incredible stress. He's learned to deal with pent-up emotions of battle. And he's become more spiritual. "You can't come to a combat zone and not develop a stronger relationship with the Lord."

Personally? "I think I'm a more sensitive person. I think I'll go back [home] and take advantage of the relationships I have with people. I've realized my own mortality." His wife and three children, aged 9, 7 and 5, "have always been the most important things in my life. Now I'll show them that they are," he said.

"Careers, success, money — all that means a whole lot less now than it did before."

A soldier's small duty

Army Spec. Duane Fawkner figures his battlefield deception helped the allies — in a small way — win the war.

Duane Fawkner — originally from the 2nd Platoon, 59th Chemical Company, 10th Mountain Division — was assigned to a small unit in the Persian Gulf.

But it had a mighty effect.

Fawkner, 20, of Napa, Calif., operated a smoke vehicle on the Kuwait border at the outset of the ground war. His job: help convince the enemy that allied forces were mustering there. "I feel that we kind of changed the battle," Fawkner said. "We lured the Iraqis down to our position. It's strange how a small platoon can do that."

The move was part of Gen. Norman Schwarzkopf's "Hail Mary" strategy that tricked the Iraqis into believing the U.S. would mount a massive ground assault from the Kuwait-Saudi border. In fact, the Allies were faking it. Most troops were sneaking in the backdoor of Kuwait through Iraq.

Fawkner said he was frightened during the battle.

"It was a natural high in a way, being scared and anticipating at the same time; it plays havoc with your mind."

He admits, though, that he was looking forward to the war. "I think everyone who comes in the service wants to go to war just a little bit. That's why everyone comes in — to be a soldier and play war."

A 1988 high school graduate, Fawkner joined the Army two years ago to earn money for a college degree. His biggest wartime worry was his mom, Janice Fawkner. A Napa radio station asked his friends and family to call in to talk about him on the air, and then sent him a tape. He couldn't bear to listen to the segment when his mom called in. "She cried every time on the tape," he said. "I fast-forward through that part."

Fawkner thinks his relationship with his mom will change now; he'll tell her everything that happened to him. "I like talking about it, to tell the truth. I'm kind of bragging about it in a way," he said. "I did something in my life that's pretty good."

A woman commander

Lt. Col. Ora J. Williams of the Quartermaster Corps was one of the first women in the U.S. Army to command a unit of both men and women.

Back in Natchez, Miss., last August for a reunion of McCullough High School, some non-military types asked Ora Williams why she was still in the Army "if you haven't made sergeant yet."

Because, she laughed, she's a lieutenant colonel — one of the highest-ranking female commanders in Operation Desert Storm. Her unit distributed food, clothing and equipment to 540,000 troops.

"Even though we're here in large numbers," she said, "the United States is not programmed to think of females in the Army. People ask me all the time, 'Are you a nurse?' And sometimes people look at me like I have no clothes on."

When she joined the armed forces 18 years ago, there were only 1,200 female officers in the Army. But about 32,400 women served in Operation Desert Storm, 6 percent of total U.S. troops. "We are here, and we are not just the powder-puff version of the soldier. We are also putting our lives on the line."

She thinks the high number of females in uniform means that "when the [women] lieutenants and captains become lieutenant colonels, they're going to be all over the place!"

For a ground-breaking Army officer, Williams had a traditional background. She was a schoolteacher for nine years after graduating with degrees in home economics and science from Alcorn State University.

But one evening, in a movie line, someone was handing out pamphlets about the U.S. Army. Right then she decided: "I wanted something different."

She got it. Williams became one of the few women ever selected for entry into the Army War College.

A soldier's Purple Heart

The ground war officially began on Feb. 23. But that didn't matter for Staff Sgt. Joseph W. Thompson.

The ground war started early for Joseph Thompson. A few days before Feb. 23, he was on a reconnaissance patrol in Iraq with his unit. They stopped to take prisoners of surrendering Iraqi soldiers. As they were marching the prisoners toward the rear, Iraqi artillery opened fire on them. They shot back.

He wasn't scared or panicked in combat. "You just do things you're supposed to do."

Suddenly Thompson, inside his Bradley Fighting Vehicle, heard an explosion. The Bradley had been hit by a Sagger anti-tank missile. The impact tore off half the turret, shattered Thompson's left knee and dislocated his shoulder. "I wasn't really sure what happened," Thompson said. He screamed to other crew members, but got no answer. The lieutenant in command was seriously wounded; the gunner dead. "I got scared after we got hit," he said. "I couldn't get my lieutenant or my gunner to answer me. I was afraid we were going to take another round."

A second Bradley crew pulled Thompson out, but he got hit in the head by flying shrapnel. Then, lying on the ground, he felt a blessed rumble — the sound of M1A1 tanks coming up to do battle with the Iraqis.

"The best thing I ever felt," he said.

Thompson's division commander awarded him a Purple Heart as he lay in a hospital bed. But Thompson doesn't see any glory in combat. "I'd rather not have seen it at all," he said when he arrived at Andrews Air Force Base, near Washington D.C. He was en route to his home base, Fort Hood, Texas. "I'd rather have sat in the desert and come home."

Now, "I look at things a little different. I don't take things for granted," he said. "Running water. You live out of a bottle over there. Simple things. You want something in the U.S., there's always a store open to go get it."

When he gets home to his wife, stepdaughter, 10, daughter, 3, and son, 2, who live in Vidor, Texas, "I'm going to go fishing." Then he's going to pour himself an

RC Cola. Or maybe a glass of iced tea.

"I missed iced tea a lot," he said. He made tea in his water bottle in the desert, but "ice was hard to come by."

A radio DJ

Chief Petty Officer Rich Yanku entertained soldiers — and boosted morale — with tunes and survival tips.

"Gooooooood mornin', Saudi Arabia!" Rich Yanku's radio debut rang out over the desert.

Yanku, 38, of Albany, N.Y., had promised he wouldn't steal Robin Williams' trademark line from the movie *Good Morning, Vietnam.* But he couldn't resist. "I liked that. I think I'll do it every morning."

The military mission of the radio service was to stem the boredom and loneliness of the troops on desert duty. Yanku was one of four broadcasters.

"We feel like we're doing a lot to help the morale of people living out in the desert, sleeping in tents, eating food out of a package. This is a touch of home," said another broadcaster, Air Force Staff Sgt. John Haynes, 27, of Phoenix.

The radio service operated much like a U.S. radio station, mixing popular songs and commercial network news. There were few limits, although broadcasters were told to avoid mentioning subjects "sensitive" to Saudi Arabia's Islamic government.

DJs offered sports updates and tips for soldiers. "Drink plenty of water; watch for snakes at sundown."

But most imporant, the DJs tried to use humor to break the tension. Yanku's first selection: "Rock the Casbah," by The Clash.

A pilot's regret

Air Force Lt. Kevin Robbins was among the first pilots deployed in the gulf war. He wouldn't have had it any other way.

As part of the 27th Tactical Fighter Squadron, "Hollywood" Robbins flew 30 air-to-air combat sorties in his F-15 — and countless more combat patrol missions.

But he never had a dogfight.

"I would have loved to have taken somebody on head to head, but [the Iraqis] had no desire whatsoever to come and fight with us," he said. "I guess that shows you the respect they had for us; they felt our presence there."

The Iraqi air force may not have wanted to tangle with the 27th Squadron. Still, the pilots had to duck lots of anti-aircraft artillery and surface-to-air missiles lobbed by the Iraqis. "Once you crossed the border, even if you didn't see anything, there was fear because you never knew what was going to happen," he said.

He admitted that training missions back home will seem tame after combat.

"Flying with your guns loaded to hilt, loaded with missiles — there's definitely something I will miss about that. But now that I know how important it is [to do it well], I'll probably train that much harder."

Robbins says it's hard for him and other pilots to grasp the enormity of their role in the war. He doesn't feel like a hero. "I think we don't even realize what we did here, because we came over here and we did our job and it just seemed pretty standard. I don't think we even really see how intimidating we were to Iraq. I guess we really have done an incredible job," he said.

Then he paused. "I don't think any of us realize that yet. That's probably a good thing."

A sympathetic captain

Safe at home in Laredo, Texas, Army Capt. Fabian Mendoza always will remember the people of Iraq.

The war may be over. But Fabian Mendoza, 33, won't soon shake his feelings of pity.

"I feel sorry for the Iraqi people, for the soldiers," he said. "It looked like they were just too devastated to fight. I feel anger toward the people who ruined Kuwait. But there are innocent people in Iraq, too. They didn't want to fight."

Mendoza, an officer with the 82nd Airborne's 20th Engineer Brigade, was based near the Saudi-Iraq border. His unit moved into Iraq, building roads and breaching minefields for combat units to make the surprise western flank sweep against the Iraqis.

"It's been real fast-paced," he said, after the fighting stopped. "It's been an adventure, but not really scary because you didn't realize what you were getting yourself into until it was almost over. It was so quick. We were kept so busy we didn't have a chance to think about what we were headed into."

Mendoza, in the Army 11 years, said the performance of the allied troops was amazing. "Our Army right now is probably the best it's ever been. We have a lot of young soldiers who are really motivated, really hard-charging and they'll take any challenge you give them."

His unit's greatest fear was chemical weapons. But Mendoza doesn't think even the use of those would have deterred them. "We talked about it. We trained for it. We were ready for it," he said. "If [Saddam] had used it, I think we still would have continued."

Mendoza thinks his wife, Yolanda, his 12-year-old daughter and 9-year-old son will notice a difference in him after the war. "I'll take a different perspective on life, that's for sure, in the way I appreciate a lot of things, the small stuff I've taken for granted. I'm going to focus more on bettering myself now that this is over with."

He'll struggle, though, with the memories of war. "There are certain things I wouldn't like to talk about, stuff we saw, lots of dead Iraqi soldiers, the prisoners."

His is the dilemma of the sympathetic soldier — the man with a duty, and a conscience. "It's our mission. They're either going to kill you or you're going to kill them. But once you get past that stage, especially after seeing what went on up there, you have to feel for those people."

A Vietnam vet

Staff Sgt. Bob Compton of Columbus, Ohio, defied his friends and family to volunteer for Operation Desert Storm.

The last time Staff Sgt. Bob Compton was this close to a shooting war, he was in the humid jungles of Vietnam.

Different place, different enemy. Same Bob Compton — 27 years later.

"I couldn't miss this one," said Compton, 45. "I've got a little experience. I want to be here and if I can help these younger guys through any war situation, then I'm going to try to help them go home."

Soldiers in his unit, the 27th Battalion of combat airborne engineers, called him "Pap."

His advice to them? Get scared, and stay that way. "I'm scared. I'm scared as hell," he said. "But that's all part of it. I don't want to get to the point that I'm not scared. Being scared keeps me on my toes and keeps that adrenaline flowing. Keeps you going in the right direction."

At 18, Compton volunteered the first time, and did a tour of duty as a paratrooper with the U.S. Army Special Forces in Vietnam. His job: rescuing downed U.S. pilots behind enemy lines, destroying U.S. planes that could not be flown out of enemy territory and "snatching" Viet Cong and North Vietnamese soldiers.

When he left the Army in 1969, he returned to a comfortable six-pack and tee-shirt life. He started a roofing business back in Ohio and drove two Harley Davidsons with MIA and American flag stickers.

Compton left active duty, but stayed with the reserves and joined the Ohio National Guard. He was still attending annual camps with the guard's 16th Engineer Brigade when Iraq invaded Kuwait.

When he found out a friend was being held hostage in Kuwait, Compton volunteered to go to Saudi Arabia. "I knew I was still fit enough to get the job done," he said.

His parents weren't very happy about it. "They don't want to see me over here because I've been through two of them," (Vietnam and Santo Domingo, where he was sent in 1965.) "They still call me the baby of the family. But I think they understand. They're proud of me."

Compton said his biker friends "would give their eyeteeth to be where I am today." He'll fill them in when he gets back.

"First thing I want to do is start up my Harley, pop a longneck [beer] and then just take off and go for a long ride across the country."

CHAPTER 5
The Home Front

A half-million troops were poised in the desert.

The deadline had passed.

And even though they knew it was coming, somehow, on Jan. 16 when the war finally began, Americans at home were surprised, a little stunned, but instantly mesmerized by the events half a world away.

They made mental notes of where they were when the news broke. They filed away the moment to stand alongside memories of the Kennedy assassination and the moon landing.

Tripp Diedrichs, a consultant, was driving home on the San Francisco Bay Bridge.

"It was another incredible San Francisco night," she said. "There are the newspaper boys with the headlines: WAR. WAR. WAR ...

"At stop lights, I looked around and everybody looked so pensive. Everybody was staring into space. You knew they were listening to the same thing you were."

Most huddled around televisions, watching the eerie, starburst images explode in the Baghdad sky. Some prayed. Others jammed phone lines, trying to get information.

As the first sketchy reports came in, elation mixed

with sadness, confusion melded with pride, fear grew amid uncertainty.

Operations Desert Shield and Desert Storm consumed the nation from the moment the first troops were ordered to Saudia Arabia in early August until hostilities ended Feb. 27. The biggest deployment of U.S. troops since Vietnam — 540,000 men and women — became a national obsession.

The war was all anyone talked about. New words and phrases entered the English language: *Scud, sortie, smart bomb, collateral damage* and the *"mother of all . . .* [fill in the blank]."

And when people weren't talking about the crisis, they were watching it on television — watching tearful mothers kiss their sons and daughters goodbye, watching troops and jeeps pour from the noses of huge C-5 cargo planes, watching reporters fumble desperately to don unwieldy gas masks.

Such scenes gave CNN its highest ratings ever, helping it march into the television big leagues. The other networks scrambled to catch up, even as CNN's Peter Arnett, Wolf Blitzer and Charles Jaco became household names.

Although it was a television war, the other media put up a good fight. Ratings for all-news radio stations soared. Newspapers printed war extras. News magazines covered almost nothing else.

Images of Saudi Arabia's parched beige desert became as familiar as the blue of a Rocky Mountain sky. But on the home front, the overriding color was yellow.

City streets and rural highways streamed with yellow ribbons. As powerful as the perennial red, white and blue, the potent symbols came in every size and permutation. Girls wore yellow-ribbon earrings; boys tied yellow ribbons around their fingers. Banks, schools, government buildings — all showed the now universal symbol of caring and support.

Not that Old Glory was forgotten. Lapels sprouted tiny die-cast flags. Dry cleaners covered freshly starched shirts with red, white and blue plastic bags. Main Street USA flowed with flags. Flapping from front porches, plastered across pickup truck windows, stuck on car bumpers, flags turned every day into Flag Day, Veterans Day and the Fourth of July combined.

Patriotism reached a fever pitch.

The war's quick execution, gee-whiz weapons and short casualty lists gave Americans plenty of reason to be proud. It had been a long time since the nation felt this good, and from the White House to the Hawaiian Islands, people seized the moment to set things right.

Said Deborah Hurt, of Pine Bluff, Ark.: "This is history in the making. We need to notice it, we need to write it in our hearts."

Watching troops march off to war will do that.

Melissa DeForest, 10, watched her daddy, Staff Sgt. Gene DeForest, ship out with 2,500 other Marines from Camp Lejeune near Jacksonville, N.C., on Aug. 7 — one of the first contingents to leave for the gulf.

"Daddy and all his friends are going to take care of it," she whispered. "Daddy is going over and kick butt."

The daddies — and mommies — did their jobs well.

But many had to leave other jobs to do it. More than 225,000 reserve and National Guard troops were activated, many for at least a year. Although only 15 percent went to the gulf, the call-up put many lives on hold back home.

San Francisco nursing student Vidal Martinez said he saw "my dreams crash away right before my eyes" when he had to quit school to deploy with his naval reserve unit. The family of USAir co-pilot Tom Lohr took an enormous pay cut when he went from flying paying passengers — earning approximately $85,000 a year — to flying Air Force transports to Saudi Arabia. "If there are any major expenses, you think twice about it," said his wife, Jennie, of Bowie, Md.

Patricia Hanvey of Tallassee, Ala., had to postpone her wedding when she had to move with her Army National Guard unit to the gulf. Countless others did the same.

But many took the opportunity to leap for the altar. Two weeks after the Iraqi invasion, 141 marriage licenses were issued in Fayetteville, N.C., near Fort Bragg, compared with 72 the year before. Similar increases were noted in other parts of the country.

Departing soldiers also made other, less joyful, arrangements. Wills were written. Guardians for children were appointed. Sperm banks got unexpected business.

Towns become ghost towns

As individuals calculated how much income they'd lose and which family milestones they'd miss, whole towns emptied.

By November, 191 men and women from the tight-knit community of Lineville, Ala., were gone, their Army National Guard units called to the gulf. In St. David, Ill., a tiny mining town of 600, the pictures of a dozen residents in the military were posted in the school window. And Killeen, Texas, home of Fort Hood — where more than half the soldiers mobilized — was a ghost town.

Walter Henderson closed his Western Sizzlin, Steak House in October, laying off 20 employees "due to Saudi." His was one of 100 businesses and 500 jobs lost in Killeen by Christmas.

Other towns paid dearly, too. In Fayetteville, N.C., Domino's Pizza saw 21 of 25 delivery drivers leave. They were soldiers moonlighting at second jobs. Verdigre, Neb., population 617, lost its only doctor when

Kenneth Pavlik was deployed. And Florence, S.C., said goodbye to 10 of its 73 police officers when they were activated.

"We miss their experience level and we miss their expertise," said Chief Ralph Porter. "And that can't be replaced."

Not all suffered, though. Con artists did a brisk business. Veterans on Long Island, N.Y., received calls from cemetery operators telling them to buy burial plots now — or risk being pushed out by the "massive" casualties of Desert Storm. Some companies offered to send $15 care packages to troops, even though the gifts cost much less.

Most businesses, though, were on the level.

Mapmakers were swamped with orders from Americans wanting to know where Kuwait was. Flag makers were flying high. Even gas-mask manufacturers saw a surge in sales as people worried over Iraq's chemical weapons threat.

In Philadelphia, some 4,000 workers went into overdrive at the Pentagon's Defense Personnel Support Center, which keeps troops supplied. At the height of the war, employees stitched more than 1,600 battle dress coats, 1,700 pairs of trousers and 700 canteen covers a day.

The sprawling, 11-block center also supplied food for the troops. The foods most popular among soldiers: "pouch bread," a roll with an 18-month shelf life, and desert chocolate bars that don't melt even at 140 degrees.

Other supplies, including goggles, sunscreen and chemical suits — 3.5 million of them — were contracted to private businesses.

One of them was McRae Industries Inc. Located in economically depressed Wadeville, N.C., the company had just laid off 130 employees because of the Cold War thaw. Desert Shield and Storm heated things up again. The company won an $8 million government contract to make 199,000 pairs of military boots and suddenly had to scramble to hire back its old workers.

"You hate to have anybody make something for a war," said Jimmy Haithcock, mayor of nearby Mount Gilead. "But somebody's got to do it, and it is a boost to the economy."

It wasn't a boom time for the national economy, however. The skyrocketing price of oil blackened everything. The stock market fell. Farmers worried about having diesel fuel for their tractors. School officials wondered how they'd heat their buildings. Business leaders became anxious as costs and layoffs rose, while pay raises shrank.

As oil inched toward $40 a barrel, consumers groaned at the gas pump. On Dec. 4, the national average for self-serve unleaded hit a high of $1.387 a gallon. It wasn't until late February that gas prices came down to pre-August levels.

"Watching the prices jump . . . was kind of scary," said Cheryl Crocker of Boone, N.C., who in September paid $1.62 a gallon instead of the usual $1.

And all the while, the recession got deeper.

"I'm terrified," said Darryl Hartley-Leonard, president of Hyatt Corp. in Chicago in September. "This is real. It is not a game. It's not crying wolf. The wolf's here this time."

But while economic woes distracted the nation's attention, war-related worries were never far behind.

Threats of terrorism on an international scale prompted changes in travel plans for thousands. Jittery tourists canceled vacations. Businesses put off employees' discretionary trips. Overseas college programs were scuttled.

More than a dozen airlines suspended service to Israel, Egypt, Jordan and Saudi Arabia. The State Department issued travel advisories for Europe and the Mideast, warning citizens to be extra careful around facilities identified as "American."

For a while, some airports were nearly deserted.

"Somebody could be carrying a bomb on board. Remember those incidents a few years ago? It could happen again," said Gustavo Martinez as he waited at Miami International Airport for a flight to Buenos Aires, Argentina. "I just hope we're safe. Things could happen any minute over there."

They did. The next day was Jan. 16, Day One of the Persian Gulf war.

The tight grip of security

The start of hostilities in the gulf brought even tighter security at home. In Texas City, Texas, side entrances were closed and employees were subjected to security checks at oil refineries and chemical plants. At the New York Stock Exchange, a swarm of guards appeared and the visitors' gallery overlooking the main trading floor was closed. Some gates at Shaw Air Force Base, S.C., were welded shut.

And in Washington, D.C., tourists were barred from the Pentagon and White House. Once the war started, those turned away could see other sights across the street from the White House in Lafayette Square. There, anti-war protesters kept a constant vigil while pounding a "peace drum."

Although polls found the vast majority of Americans supported President Bush's gulf policy, thousands of anti-war protesters marched to a different beat, many shouting "No Blood for Oil!" Among the most active was Alex Molnar, founder of the Military Families Support Network. "We're a pro-America movement," said Molnar, whose son served in the gulf. "The principal concern of the U.S. government should be the welfare of [U.S.] people. We don't say no war, ever. We just say this [war] is bad policy."

In San Francisco, the city which drew the most sustained protests, thousands were arrested when demonstrators shut down the Bay Bridge, forced the closure of the federal building and blocked downtown streets. Protest-related vandalism was rife. In Washington, D.C., more than 75,000 people marched Jan. 26 in what was to be the largest protest of the war. After that sizable turnout, the movement seemed to fizzle.

A handful of conscientious objectors refused to report for duty. San Francisco declared itself a sanctuary for objectors, one of whom was Liann Noble. Said the Army National Guard member: "The thought of any kind of violence disgusts me. . . . When I joined three years ago, it seemed impossible I'd be in the midst of the horrors of war."

Unlike Vietnam War protesters, gulf dissidents said they supported U.S. troops, even while opposing their mission.

Some didn't buy that. "I think we should put the protesters on a plane and send them to Iraq," said Helen Taylor of Virginia Beach, Va., a military town whose residents came out to heckle anti-war demonstrators near city hall.

Joe Baden, a Vietnam veteran, had even harsher words for protesters: "They're giving aid and comfort to the enemy."

Perhaps the most telling signs of how the nation had changed since Vietnam were on college campuses. Students may have fretted about the possibility of a draft, but most — just like their parents — supported the administration's policy.

That was even true at Ohio's Kent State University, where four student protesters were killed by National Guardsmen on May 4, 1970. Once a bellwether of anti-war feeling, Kent State now harbored a new breed of activist, resentful of the school's history and supportive of the gulf war.

"There's a strong American voice here," said Mike Homula, a founder of United Students for the Liberation of Kuwait. "I think it's time we stopped living in the past and started looking to the future."

The nation's 2.6 million Vietnam veterans also saw the gulf war as a chance to stop living in the past. Although for some it brought flashbacks of emotions long buried, for others it raised hopes of re-enlisting to fight in a winnable war.

"Vietnam veterans are feeling very glad about the fact that there seems to be popular support for the troops," said Paul Egan of Vietnam Veterans of America. "But there's jealousy about that."

Said Vietnam veteran Craig Clark: "They called us baby-killers and all that stuff and we were just doing what they [superiors] told us to do. Nobody wants to be in a war you know you can't win. But in this one, you do have the American public behind you."

Conflict divides the nation

Like other Americans, Jews were horrified by Saddam Hussein's threats to attack Israel. Hours before the war began, 400 Yeshiva University students left New York on a chartered plane for Israel. Their goal: to show support for the Jewish state.

"It's my homeland. They're my brethren," said Aliza Rachlin, 20, of Memphis, Tenn. "I don't think it's an alternative to let them fight alone."

Among the nation's 3 million Arab-Americans, reports of anti-Arab threats, beatings, vandalism and harassment skyrocketed after Iraq's Aug. 2 invasion of Kuwait. And it didn't matter if the target wasn't an Iraqi.

Robert Haddoni is Lebanese. Yet his Detroit home was splattered with graffiti and then firebombed. "I'm being blamed for something I had nothing to do with," Haddoni said.

A USA TODAY poll of Arab-Americans showed that while two-thirds supported U.S. policy, the war proved "the most divisive crisis ever faced," said Kahalil Jahshan of the National Association of Arab Americans. "There are people in our community who have worked together for years who no longer talk to each other as a result of this. It has been very intense."

In one widely condemned move, the FBI in January announced a plan to interview 200 Arab-American business and community leaders to learn about possible terrorist activities. The program was billed as an effort to fight anti-Arab backlash and protect Arab-Americans, but critics said it would leave a smear — "that by nature of our ethnicity . . . we should know about terrorists," said Albert Mokhiber of the Arab-American Anti-Discrimination Committee.

Despite the positive image of Joint Chiefs of Staff Chairman Colin Powell, some black leaders — though not Powell — complained that blacks made up a disproportionate number of the volunteer forces in the gulf. Almost 30 percent of Army gulf personnel were black, compared with just 12 percent of blacks in the general population.

"I'm offended by the extraordinary disproportion of blacks," said Washington, D.C., congressional representative Eleanor Holmes Norton. "I think it unseemly that a largely white country would be defended so disproportionately in the event of war."

No matter what their race, no families were touched more by the war than those who had loved ones serving in the gulf. Many lived with the daily fear that an officer would knock on the door, bearing the worst of news.

Wives and husbands met in support groups to trade coping tips and share rumors. Hot lines were set up to solve financial problems. Birthing coaches were found for many of the women who delivered nearly 7,000 babies while their husbands were away.

A lot of children sent homework assignments and drawings to parents in Saudi Arabia. Schools and offices sent cookies, batteries, Christmas trees and valentines. More than 40 million pounds of mail were sent before the ground war began — 15 percent of it addressed to "Any Service Member." Much of it was written by children who'd heard about the war on television, at playgrounds and, often, at home.

Children have to say goodbye

Tens of thousands of children watched a parent go off to war; 16,337 of the soldiers in the gulf were single parents. In 1,231 families, both parents went off to war, reflecting the new and increasingly active role of women in the military.

For young children left behind, the war was mysterious and exciting. Most of all, though, it was painful.

"It's a state of chronic sorrow or grief," said Tucson psychologist Dennis Embry, who counseled Desert Storm children and wrote a book just for them. "It's as if their parent is slowly dying, and now, it's as if that death could be really quick. There is lots of anger and sadness."

Although military parents are required to have a child-care plan, it didn't always work out as expected. There were the West Virginia children left by their military parents in the care of a woman charged with murdering her husband. There was the Tennessee single father who left his three children, ages 13, 12 and 10, home alone with a note telling how to use the automatic bank-teller card. There was the Virginia reservist called up two weeks after the birth of her son.

Such stories — along with images of orphaned children — focused attention on the record 32,400 women serving in the gulf, 6 percent of all the forces there.

Feminists, conservatives, military analysts, child-care experts and just plain folks waged an endless debate on the role of women, particularly mothers, in the military.

"In a war, you don't know where combat will occur," said Lawrence Korb, former assistant defense secretary for manpower, installations and logistics.

He was right. Three women died in a Scud missile attack in a rear area near Dhahran. Another perished when her support helicopter went down after the cease-fire. Another died stepping on a land mine. None was in a combat job, legally barred to women.

Although none of these dead was a mother, the argument raged. "I don't think [mothers] ought to be leaving their children," said Boston pediatrician T. Berry Brazelton, author of *Infants and Mothers*. The child "may begin to think, 'My mommy doesn't love me or why would she go away?'"

But retired Army Brig. Gen. Pat Foote doesn't believe in exceptions: "You just don't pull out people and give them preferential status" because they are parents.

Pediatrician Gwen Wurm of the University of Miami School of Medicine agreed. "A mother coming back in a body bag is as bad as a man coming back in a body bag. They're both going to be traumatic."

And in towns with names like Rochester Mills, Pa., and Navarre, Fla., it was.

In tiny Rochester Mills, where Christine Mayes grew up along the rushing Little Mahoning Creek, neighbors sat silently in the family's living room as they pondered how a Scud missile could end a life at 22. Said Christine's mother, Darlene, "This is just something that happened that you never expect, but this time it hit home."

The day Air Force Capt. Arthur Galvan and 13 other crew members of a downed AC-130 gunship were listed as missing [and believed dead], his son, Jason, a fifth-grader, went to school. After telling classmates what had happened, "He got his books and said he wouldn't be at school for a few days," said Santa Rosa County School Superintendent Benny Russell. "He apparently handled it very courageously, very maturely."

So, in the end, did the country.

CHAPTER 6

Those Who Died

Every one of them was a hero, said Gen. Norman Schwarzkopf, of the returning prisoners of war. What words, then, can adequately honor those who gave their lives?

From August to early March, 322 service men and women died while assigned to Operations Desert Shield and Desert Storm. As of March 8, 10 were still missing in action.

Many — roughly half, in fact — died in training exercises and accidents. Despite its inevitability, it's the dearest price of moving a population as large as that of the entire state of Alaska or the city of Cleveland to hostile land and water thousands of miles away from home.

Ironies abound. There are people who were one mission from retirement, who were transferred into danger at the last minute, who died without seeing new babies.

All were duty-bound military. But they were also fathers and mothers, Sunday School teachers, Little League umpires, former high school track stars and yearbook editors. And they were beloved. "Our lives can never be the same," said one widow.

In these brief capsules, we have tried to hint at the loss, at the personal worlds these men and women inhabited far away from the missiles and bombs in the desert sand.

For some, we've listed surviving family. For others, we used the space for personal quotes or memories. Stories are drawn from staff reports, the Associated Press and local newspapers.

A book ten times this size, filled entirely with tributes to these soldiers, would not be enough to contain their stories. Or to fill the spaces they left.

THOMAS R. ADAMS, 20
Marine Lance Cpl.; Baton Rouge, La.

Nothing bothered Adams, said sister Tara of the man who "always knew how to make you smile." When her daughter was born, she named Adams godfather. And like so many others, Adams loved to fish, hunt and work on old cars. He and his dad had put a new engine in Adams' 1979 Dodge before he shipped out.

When Adams joined the Marines, he became a helicopter mechanic, fell in love with flying and volunteered to train as a door gunner. On Oct. 8, he was among eight Marines killed in a helicopter collision over the Arabian Sea. Had he returned, the family would have had a reunion at his younger brother's graduation from a Navy training school in Florida. The brothers "were going to compare boot camp experiences," said his mother.

Before he left, he met Kim Wilkey in a California dance club. They exchanged letters. His parents flew her to Baton Rouge for his funeral. Said his mother: "The church was full. There must have been 200 or 300 there."

ANDY ALANIZ, 20
Army Pfc.; Corpus Christi, Texas

A member of the 24th Infantry, Alaniz was killed Feb. 27 when his tank ran over a land mine in Iraq. A local

Texas priest described him as someone who never liked anyone to be sad, even over bad grades. At Moody High, where he graduated in 1989, he played baseball and took part in school plays. And he was good at it. Said drama teacher Sherri Davis: "The acting talent he had came from within, because I think he had such a good heart."

FRANK C. ALLEN, 22
Marine Lance Cpl.; Waianae, Hawaii

Allen liked surfing, movies, reggae music and concerts. He was part shy, part rascal, said best friend David Haji.

Allen and four other Marines died Jan. 29 when their light armored vehicle was struck by a missile in the Saudi border town of Khafji.

Born on Okinawa, he graduated from Roosevelt High School in Honolulu in 1986. He moved to Oceanside, Calif., when he joined the Marines in 1988.

MICHAEL R. ALLEN, 31
Army Staff Sgt.; Fort Bragg, N.C.

A member of the XVIIIth Airborne Corps, the 11-year veteran, a communications expert, died of an apparent heart attack on Feb. 25.

DAVID R. AMES, 30
Army Staff Sgt.; Schuyler, N.Y.

Tank mechanic Ames, father of two, was killed in action Feb. 19. "He achieved all his goals — raising the family and being the best in the Army," said his widow, Cindy.

MICHAEL F. ANDERSON, 36
Army Chief Warrant Officer; Frankfort, Ind.

He knew the Declaration of Independence by heart. He was "Chuck Norris, Clint Eastwood and John Wayne all rolled into one," said his father. The helicopter pilot died during a non-combat crash after picking up injured soldiers during a medical evacuation. Anderson, married and the father of three, had flown combat missions in Grenada and earned a Purple Heart in Panama.

TONY R. APPLEGATE, 28
Army Sgt.; Portsmouth, Ohio

Portsmouth's "soldiers' tree," decorated with hundreds of orange light bulbs and wooden name tags, bore a black ribbon for Applegate, the first local soldier to die in the war. The father of two was killed Feb. 27 when his tank was hit by enemy fire. His sister, Debbie, recalled he enjoyed sports and played basketball and football in high school. "He was always gung-ho about everything he wanted."

JORGE I. ARTEAGA, 26
Air Force 1st Lt.; Trumbull, Conn.

Arteaga and Emily Gardner married Jan. 14, in Blytheville, Ark., just two hours before he shipped out. Emily said he wanted to make sure she was covered by military benefits if anything happened to him.

He was educated in Spain, Brazil and the U.S.A. and spoke four languages. An Air Force navigator, he died Feb. 2 when his B-52 bomber crashed in the Indian Ocean.

IMAGES OF WAR

People who faced the Persian Gulf crisis

HELD HOSTAGE: Saddam Hussein with British hostage Stuart Lockwood, 5

MOVING OUT: U.S. 1st Cavalry Division marches in Saudi desert as diplomats negotiated to avert war.

By Eileen Blass, USA TODAY

GODSPEED: Clementine Henderson kisses her husband, Sgt. John Henderson, in a Cumberland, Md., parade.

By Dave Martin, AP

GOODBYE: Belinda Holyfield holds her son Marcus for a tearful farewell.

TALKING TURKEY: President Bush shares a Thanksgiving feast during his visit with the troops in Saudi Arabia.

By Sadayuki Mikami, AP

TRAINING FOR WAR: Marines sweep Iraqi-style trenches in Saudi Arabia during tense weeks before war.

By Charles Platiau, Bettmann Archives

LONELY WAIT: Marine Lance Corporal Keith Lamont Dorsette, Brooklyn, N.Y., plays a sax serenade near front.

By Porter Binks, USA TODAY

PASSING THE TIME: Army Pfc. Robert McCann, 19, Butte, Mont., reads atop overturned tank during war buildup.

By Bob Daugherty, AP

STANDING OUT: General H. Norman Schwarzkopf — the 6-foot-3, 230-pound "Bear" — visits the troops.

AP

PEP TALK: General Colin Powell rallies the troops in Saudi Arabia.

By Mark Peters, SIPA

THUMBS UP: A Marine reserve pilot prepares his F-4 Phantom for takeoff in the first wave of bombing sorties into Iraq.

By Gill Allen, AP

MISSION COMPLETED: Cheering ground crewmen wave in an F-16 fighter plane after a successful bombing mission.

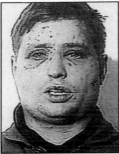

Iraqi TV

CAPTURED: Navy Lt. Jeffrey Zaun's shocking TV image

Bettmann Archives

RELEASED: Zaun 43 days later after his release in Baghdad

TAKING COVER: Two Marines huddle behind a wall during an Iraqi artillery attack on Saudi border town of Khafji.

By John Giordano, SABA

HI-TECH PATRIOTS: Capt. James Spangler led the Patriot crew intercepting Iraqi Scuds.

By Dennis Brack, Black Star

ON THE MOVE: Saudi troops move along a cleared track toward Kuwait City during the first days of ground war.

By David Turnley, Black Star

A SOLDIER'S SORROW: Al Kozakiewicz, 23, of Buffalo, N.Y., mourns the death of a fellow tank crewman.

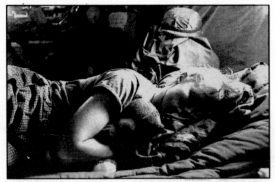

SWEET DREAMS: Nurse Amy Stuart naps (read her story in Chapter 2)

GRIEF: Gayle Edwards comforts her children at their father's funeral, the war's first in Arlington National Cemetery.

By Joe DeVera, USA TODAY

CLEANING UP: Army troops blow up Iraqi ammo truck after the battle of Euphrates Valley.

By Joe DeVera, USA TODAY

ROAD TO HELL: Allied soldier inspects remains of Iraqi tank destroyed in the Convoy of Death out of Kuwait.

By Sadayuki Mikami, AP

CHEERS: Kuwaitis hail Egyptian convoy in Kuwait City.

By Laurent Rebours, AP

LIBERATION: Jubilant Kuwaitis mob a U.S. special forces soldier after Iraqi forces were routed.

By Sadayuki Mikami, AP

FREEDOM: Former POW Army Maj. Rhonda Cornum arrives at Riyadh.

By Rob Jordan, AP

GOING HOME: Victory signs abound as members of the 24th Mechanized Infantry Division leave Dhahran.

By Eileen Blass, USA TODAY

SWEET HOMECOMING: A hug from Mom for Scott Barberides

By Christopher Morris, Black Star

SEMPER FIDELIS: U.S. Marine carries the American flag across the desert sands near the Saudi-Kuwaiti border.

STEVEN ATHERTON, 25
Army Spec.; Dayton, Pa.

Atherton's main ambition was to buy a house for his wife, Brenda, and young son, Aaron. "He spent most of his time with his family, he seemed to enjoy that more than anything else," said his cousin, Earl Atherton. "Anytime you would see Steve, he would have a smile on his face and was out to do something. He wasn't the type to sit around." Atherton was killed Feb. 25 in the Al-Khobar Scud attack.

HANS CHRISTIAN RICHARD AVEY, 21
Army Pvt.; Falls Church, Va.

A military policeman, Avey died Jan. 7 in a truck accident in Saudi Arabia.

STANLEY W. BARTUSIAK, 34
Army Spec.; Columbia, Tenn.

Bartusiak was always up, said his mother. "You just couldn't make him down." Once a few years back, Bartusiak donned a Beatles wig and drove to the local mall with his brother, Paul — all to make onlookers laugh. "People need to smile," he said.

Remarried in January shortly after receiving his military orders, Bartusiak had two children from his previous marriage.

On March 4, his mother, Irene, received his last letter — written the same day Bartusiak died in a Scud missile attack. Everything was fine, he wrote. He was playing a lot of Monopoly and cards and drinking too much coffee. "We're not in any danger," the letter said, "except for Scuds."

TOMMIE BATES, 27
Army 1st. Lt.; Coventry, R.I.

A 1986 West Point graduate, Bates was killed in a Sept. 14 truck accident in Dhahran. "You would have had to meet him to appreciate the life that he had within him," said his high school principal. A writer, a cross-country runner, a student council member, "he was an All-American type." Bates joined the Army in 1981, then won an appointment to West Point. Three of his four brothers also serve in the Army.

CINDY M. BEAUDOIN, 19
Army Spec.; Plainfield, Conn.

Beaudoin had a grandmother "she loved very much who passed away of cancer just a few years ago, and Cindy nursed her until she died," recalled an uncle. "That's when she realized she wanted to help people for her career." Two years ago, Beaudoin joined the 142nd Medical Company of the National Guard, which taught her medicine and paid her freshman tuition at the University of Connecticut.

"She was caring and carefree," said best friend Kerry Menacho. She danced to relax and passed long hours at the beach. "Soon we'll be together again at the shore, in the sun," Beaudoin wrote from Saudi Arabia. Beaudoin died Feb. 28 after stepping on a land mine in Kuwait as she went to help a fallen soldier.

LEE A. BELAS, 22
Army Sgt.; Port Orchard, Wash.

Belas had an ear for languages. After high school, he went to Belgium, where he studied German, Latin and

Dutch. "He referred to it as his fantasy year, and it's when he fell in love with languages," his mother said. Back in the States, he joined military intelligence. The Army taught him Russian, French and Arabic.

In Saudi Arabia, as an electronic warfare voice interpreter, Belas rode in a Blackhawk helicopter, listening for enemy transmissions and jamming them.

Belas liked to read science fiction and spy novels; he recently finished *The Russia House*. Someday, he told his mother, he wanted to be an ambassador.

In his last call home, his mother said, Belas marveled at the camels that often ran through his desert camp. His helicopter was shot down Feb. 27 in enemy territory.

MICHAEL L. BELLIVEAU, 24
Navy Petty Officer; Lakewood, Colo.

He and 20 other sailors died Dec. 22 when a ferry bringing them back from leave in Israel capsized in the Mediterranean Sea.

STEPHEN E. BENTZLIN, 23
Marine Cpl.; Wood Lake, Minn.

Bentzlin's mother, Barbara Anderson, spoke to a rally in St. Paul the day after the ground war started. She recalled her son writing and telling her, "If we're going to go, let's go full force."

He spoke to Carol, his wife of 13 months, a week before his death. "He wanted to talk about details should he not return. He tried to prepare me for this. He said, 'Somebody's gonna get hurt, Babe.' But I didn't believe it would be Steve." Bentzlin, the first of the Sisseton-Wahpeton Sioux tribe to die, was killed Jan. 29 when a U.S. missile accidentally hit his armored vehicle.

KURTIS A. BENZ, 22
Marine Cpl.; Garden City, Mich.

"He was a big jokester," recalled his 18-year-old sister, Kim. "I'll always remember his smile." Benz, who died Feb. 2 when his helicopter crashed in Saudi Arabia, joined the Marines after graduating from high school because "they're the best. He always wanted to be the best," she said.

DENNIS W. BETZ, 22
Marine Sgt.; Alliance, Ohio

"He liked living on the edge," said his father, Roger. A good bunter, Betz played catcher for the Reese Body Shop baseball team that went 22-0 and won the state 'F' league championship for boys 13-15.

Betz decided to become a Marine after watching his brother — a Marine drill instructor — graduate from boot camp. He was part of the secret "FAST (Fleet Anti-Terrorist Support Team) Company," which reportedly was in Panama before the 1989 invasion.

Betz headed a 22-man machine gun section that left for the gulf Aug. 7. He fell ill on the USS *Guam* and died Dec. 9 of a brain hemorrhage. He had hoped to leave the Marines in 1992 to join the police department SWAT team in Pensacola, Fla.

He left a long letter to be opened if he died. It said: "Don't blame the Marine Corps."

SCOTT F. BIANCO, 21
Marine Cpl.; Troy, Mo.

Bianco and two buddies graduated from Edwardsville High School in 1987 and joined the Marines.

His wife, Diane, said he asked to be sent to the gulf because he didn't want to stay home when his friends were in harm's way. Attached to the Marine's 1st Landing Support Battalion, Bianco was operating a forklift on Feb. 17, unloading a ship in a Saudi port, when his vehicle plunged into the water.

He'd last phoned his wife three days earlier — on Valentine's Day.

THOMAS CLIFFORD BLAND, JR., 26
Air Force 1st Lt.; Fort Walton Beach, Fla.

Listed as MIA, Bland was a crew member of an Air Force gunship that crashed Jan. 31 in waters off Kuwait. All crewmen were believed to be dead. A photograph of him is proudly displayed at his mother's restaurant, Dede's Diner, in Gaithersburg, Md.

JOHN P. BLESSINGER, 33
Air Force Staff Sgt.; Fort Walton Beach, Fla.

He is also believed to have been killed in the Jan. 31 plane crash in the gulf. Said neighbor Raymond Condren: "He was a true, dedicated airman — someone who is very hard to find these days."

TOMMY BLUE, 33
Army Sgt.; Spring Lake, N.C.

Blue, a cook, died of a heart attack Dec. 30 in Saudi Arabia. He was buried at Fort Bragg, N.C.

JEFFREY J. BNOSKY, 25
Army Capt.; Hometown, Pa.

Bnosky, with Company D of the 5th Engineer Battalion, was the first to leave Fort Leonard Wood, Mo., for Operation Desert Shield.

"We were different than most [fathers and sons] because we were like best friends," said his father, Joseph. "I started him off [riding motorbikes] when he was 8 or 9. Four kids had their own little motorcycle club. Three of them are dead now. One died of cancer, another fell off a cliff when he was camping. They all had silk-screened T-shirts that said 'Hometown Dirt Riders.'"

Bnosky died Jan. 13 when a Humvee he was riding in collided with a military tractor-trailer in Saudi Arabia. His promotion to captain from a first lieutenant came two days later.

JOHN BOLIVER, JR., 27
Army Spec.; Monongahela, Pa.

He joined the Army reserves on Aug. 2, unaware that Saddam Hussein's forces had invaded Kuwait. He died in a Scud attack two days before President Bush called for a cease-fire. In November, the Bolivers and their two children were settling into their new house when he was activated.

JOSEPH P. BONGIORNI III, 20
Army Spec.; Hickory, Pa.

"He was very patriotic. We had to fly the flag," said his mother, Rita. He had been in Saudi Arabia five days before he died in a Scud attack Feb. 25. His parents said they discouraged their color-blind son from volunteering for desert duty. "He was just a very good boy, very good. This was the only time he didn't listen to us," she said.

JOHN T. BOXLER, 44
Army Sgt.; Johnstown, Pa.

Boxler was a Little League volunteer, a fire fighter and emergency medical technician who loved to cook. This was his second tour of duty in a war zone; the first was Vietnam. He re-enlisted, thinking "if he goes over there it might save some young kid from getting killed," said his younger brother. He died in a Scud attack.

WILLIAM C. BRACE, 24
Army Spec.; Fountain Hill, Pa.

Cars were his passion. Brace spent hours tinkering with car engines or hanging out at a nearby speedway. In the Army, he was a mechanic and crew chief of a Chinook helicopter that crashed in northern Saudi Arabia March 2. His helicopter was returning to base after dropping off Iraqi prisoners of war when it hit a tower. Brace had been in the gulf since August, four weeks after his wife gave birth to their first child — a son named William Arthur Carl, after his father and grandfather. The last time Brace called his dad was just before the war: "He was a little bored over there, but said things were getting busier."

DOUGLAS LLOYD BRADT, 29
Air Force Capt.; Houston, Texas

Bradt, who grew up near Johnson Space Center, got the flying lessons he begged for as a sixteenth birthday present. He was killed Feb. 14 when his radar-jamming

EF-111 Raven went down in Saudi Arabia after a combat mission. At his funeral at Fort Sam Houston National Cemetery, four F-111 fighter bombers flew in a "missing man" formation.

ROGER P. BRILINSKI, JR., 24
Army Sgt.; Ossineke, Mich.

On Feb. 27 Brilinski volunteered to accompany a Blackhawk helicopter crew that went behind enemy lines to rescue a downed F-16 pilot. He was killed by Iraqi anti-aircraft fire.

"The last mail I got from him was a valentine," said his mother, Judy. "He wanted to tell me he loved me."

TYRONE BROOKS, 19
Navy Boiler Tech.; Detroit, Mich.

Brooks saw the Navy as a job opportunity and a "chance to become a man, quick," said his uncle, Samuel Bracey. He was killed Oct. 30 in a boiler room explosion on the USS *Iwo Jima.*

CHRISTOPHER B. BROWN, 19
Navy Airman Apprentice; Leslie, Ga.

Brown's mom was a single parent of four children and he was the oldest. "The other kids looked up to Christopher like a father and he was our backbone when his brother was dying of leukemia in 1988," she said. "He was always trying to keep our spirits up." Brown, who joined the Navy after high school graduation, died with 20 other sailors when their ferry capsized in the Mediterranean Sea returning from Christmas leave in Israel.

DARRELL K. BROWN, 19
Navy Airman Apprentice; Memphis, Tenn.

Wanting to learn a trade, Brown joined the Navy shortly after graduation. He hoped to work one day for the Federal Express Corp. "He was a small fellow, but he had a big heart," said his father. Brown died on the ferry that capsized Dec. 22, in the Mediterranean Sea.

JAMES R. BROWN, 27
Army Spec.; Pittsburgh, Pa.

Brown died Jan. 22 from injuries sustained in an earlier vehicle accident. He died while being transported to the United States.

PAUL G. BUEGE, 43
Air Force Senior Master Sgt.; Mary Esther, Fla.

Listed as MIA, Buege was a crew member of an Air Force gunship that crashed Jan. 31 off Kuwait. All crew members were believed to have died.

TOMMY D. BUTLER, 22
Army Spec.; Amarillo, Texas

Butler, who had been stationed in Fort Sill, Okla., was killed March 1 by a bomblet explosion. A sports fanatic and a comedian, he always made everybody laugh. His father said Butler's "death was not a personal thing because he was doing it for all of us, not just for me and his mother."

WILLIAM T. BUTTS, 30
Army Staff Sgt.; Enterprise, Ala.

Although he loved flying, Butts' pet love was motorcycles and dirt bikes, which he used to take apart and put back together from memory. Butts was with an eight-member crew of a Blackhawk helicopter attempting to rescue a downed pilot when his craft crashed Feb. 27.

ANDREW T. CADY, 25
Navy Petty Officer; San Diego, Calif.

Cady joined the Navy after his junior year in high school. He was an air crewman on the USS *Tripoli*, and died Dec. 19 en route to the gulf when his helicopter crashed during a night training mission off Guam.

THOMAS R. CALDWELL, 32
Air Force Capt.; Columbus, Ohio

Although he lived with his wife in England, where he was stationed, Caldwell was a loyal Ohio State University football fan. His mother taped games of his alma mater and the Cleveland Browns. He was killed Oct. 10 when his F-111 bomber crashed during a training exercise.

KEVIN LEE CALLOWAY, 20
Army Pfc.; Arpin, Wis.

Next-door neighbor Jim Berghammer said this of Calloway: He "was a real gentle person. You know when a cow is laying down in the barn and he doesn't want to get up, so you've got to kick him or slap him? Well, Kevin wouldn't do that. He didn't want to hurt the cow."

Calloway was killed in a truck accident Nov. 24 in the Saudi desert.

JOHN CAMPISI, 30
Air Force Staff Sgt.; Covina, Calif.

He was the first Desert Shield fatality.

On Aug. 12, the aircraft maintenance technician was sitting on a dark runway in Saudi Arabia, waiting for a flight crew, when a truck struck him.

"He's the one we called the peacemaker," a friend remembered. "His patience and caring always got everyone through the hard and difficult times."

Campisi joined the Air Force at 18 and served in the Philippines and Korea. Off duty, he coached soccer and taught Catholic catechism classes. "His hobbies," his father said, "were his kids."

On Aug. 8, with two hours' notice, Campisi shipped out for the gulf. He had 45 minutes to spend with his wife and no time to say goodbye to his four children.

JASON C. CARR, 24
Army Sgt.; Halifax, Va.

His family planned to scatter his ashes over the Blue Ridge Mountains near Lynchburg, where he played as a boy, his father said. Carr loved fishing, hunting and hiking. A tactical transport helicopter repairman who had advanced to crew chief, Carr was killed Feb. 27 when his helicopter was shot down.

MONRAY C. CARRINGTON, 22
Navy Seaman; North Braddock, Pa.

Carrington had no illusions about the dangers of military service; five of his brothers and sisters had served before he enlisted in the Navy in 1987. He was the only one to die in the service, though. A ferry capsized while taking him back to the USS *Saratoga* after Christmas leave in Israel. "I feel like a part of me left when he left," said his twin brother, Raymon. "My heart aches."

CLARENCE ALLEN CASH, 20
Army Spec.; Ashland, Ohio

Cash liked deer hunting and target shooting, said his wife, Sandy. The two had known each other 12 years before marrying a year ago. "He was just hyper," as a child, she said. "He never could sit still." A member of the 3rd Infantry Division, Cash was killed in combat Feb. 26.

CHRISTOPHER J. CHAPMAN, 25
Army Sgt.; Charlotte, N.C.

An ROTC student at West Charlotte High, Chapman enlisted after graduating and became a paratrooper with the 82nd Airborne. But he could not resist the lure of the "Night Stalkers," the 160th Special Operations Aviation Regiment, with its high-tech equipment and secrecy. Blackhawk helicopters and highly classified night-flying operations thrilled the inquisitive Chapman, who as a child conducted his own study of electricity by inserting a screwdriver into a wall socket (with explosive but non-lethal results). Chapman died Feb. 21 when the helicopter on which he was crew chief crashed in bad weather during a medical evacuation mission.

RICHARD W. CHASE, 43
Air Force Maj.; San Antonio, Texas

The former general manager of Kelly Air Force Base was one of 13 killed aboard a cargo plane that crashed at Ramstein Air Force Base in Germany en route to the gulf in late August.

MICHAEL L. CHINBURG, 26
Air Force Capt.; Durham, N.H.

A graduate of the University of Colorado, Chinburg joined the Air Force in March 1987. Before heading overseas, Chinburg told his brother, Eric, that he knew he might not come home, but that he already had lived a lifetime of happiness since his September wedding to April Sloane. Chinburg died Jan. 8 when his F-16 crashed in Saudi Arabia.

BARRY CLARK, 26
Army Sgt.; Hurlburt Field, Fla.

Listed as MIA, he was aboard an Air Force gunship that crashed Jan. 31. All crewmen were believed to be dead.

BEVERLY CLARK, 23
Army Spec.; Armagh, Pa.

Co-workers remember Clark as the woman with the perpetual smile. "She was so full of energy and life," said Georgia Lightcap of Season-All, a storm window and door company in Indiana, Pa., where Clark worked as a quality assurance coordinator.

The reservist loved athletics — jogging with her sister, playing volleyball on the company team, entering cheerleading competitions. In high school she earned varsity letters in volleyball, basketball and softball.

Bank teller Karen Fry waited on Clark the day she was called to duty. "She was shaking," said Fry, whose son is a Marine in the gulf. "I grabbed her hand and squeezed it real hard and said, 'Good luck.'"

Clark died in the Feb. 25 Scud missile attack.

LARRY M. CLARK, 21
Navy Airman; Decatur, Ga.

Clark sent roses and a birthday card to his 3-year-old daughter, Tiffany, which arrived the same weekend as the news of his death. "I want to wrap you up in hugs," he wrote. "If anything happens to me before that day, remember Daddy loves you very much." Clark was nicknamed "Boombox" because he talked all of the time, said his father. He was killed Dec. 22 when the ferry bringing him back from leave capsized.

OTTO F. CLARK, 35
Army Sgt.; Corinth, N.Y.

At his memorial service — packed with his neighbors from his small upstate town — Clark's widow, Dawn, was presented a Purple Heart. The medic was killed Feb. 21 in a helicopter that crashed in bad weather while on an evacuation mission. His father said, "When they played taps, to me that was it. I'd rather forget. He liked what he was doing, and that's all there is to it."

STEPHEN DOUGLAS CLARK, 22
Army Spec.; Cedar Rapids, Iowa

Clark was crushed in a truck accident in the desert Nov. 7. He graduated from Cedar Rapids Prairie High School in 1986 and joined the Army a year later.

After his death, his mother received a letter mailed before the accident: "Mom, it's really bad over here. What I wouldn't give for a piece of your pumpkin pie and ice cream."

MARC CLEYMAN, 30
Air Force Staff Sgt.; Jacksonville Beach, Fla.

Assigned to West Germany, Cleyman met aunts and uncles — living in Belgium and The Netherlands — for the first time. "He just loved his work," said his mother, Jeanine. "The people, the travel and feeling like he was doing something." Cleymen died in the late August crash of a gulf-bound cargo plane in Germany.

GERARD A. COHEN, 30
Army Spec.; St. Louis, Mo.

A month before he died, Cohen told his mother: "Mom, don't worry. We're winners." Cohen had hoped to become a Baptist minister. He died Feb. 28 in a truck-loading accident.

MELFORD R. COLLINS, 34
Army Pfc.; Uhland, Texas

"If you were feeling down, he'd be there with a smile. If you had a problem, he'd be there to solve it," said Collins' sister. Three years ago, Collins' wife became ill. The family couldn't afford the medical bills; the Army could. So Collins enlisted — for a second time — at age 31.

He broke his hand last year working in the motor pool. The Army wasn't going to send him to the gulf, so he broke off the cast early and insisted that he was ready. Born in Muleshoe, Texas, the fuel-truck driver was killed by a land mine Feb. 24.

MARK A. CONNELLY, 34
Army Maj.; Manheim Township, Pa.

After he went to Lancaster General Hospital to teach in the family practice residency program in 1989, Connelly and another doctor created an "E (for encouragement) Team" as a support group for friends who also were dads. And when his daughter, Meggan, brought home a note from her softball coach asking for adult volunteers, he was there the next day, coaching third base.

Connelly, the father of two, died Feb. 28 when the vehicle he was driving struck a land mine as he went to aid surrendering Iraqi soldiers. When the incident was reported — before the victims' names were announced — Lancaster hospital spokesman Wally Hudson said people there were saying, "Oh, my God, that sounds like something Mark would do."

Friends looked to him as a perfect father, so they created a scholarship fund in his children's names.

MICHAEL R. CONNER, 32
Army Spec.; Plainfield, Conn.

Conner died in late January in an armored vehicle collision in Saudi Arabia. "I learned you only get one chance at meaningful things. . . . That's why for the last few years I purposely stopped to smell the roses, watch children play," he wrote his sister, Michelle Sakara, a month before he died.

MICHAEL D. COOKE, 22
Marine Cpl.; Willow Grove, Pa.

Cooke had asked his mother to stay composed if officers came to her door bearing bad news. He died in February when a grenade accidentally exploded as he cleaned his gear after a mission. When the officers showed up, Joan Cooke cried but "just stood there." She wanted to perform the way her son expected her to.

ARDON BRAD COOPER, 23
Army Pfc.; Seattle, Wash.

A big homecoming party was planned for Cooper's discharge in May. Instead, he died Feb. 20 when enemy fire hit his anti-aircraft vehicle.

Friend Rodger Schnee said that once Cooper arrived in Saudi Arabia, "he did a lot of soul-searching. He wrote about how important what you've got seems to be when it's threatened."

CHARLES W. COOPER, 33
Army Capt.; St. Charles, Ill.

Cooper used his college degree in criminal justice to become a police intern, but no one was surprised when he enlisted in the Army. Said a friend: "He liked challenges and confrontations. He was gregarious and flamboyant, yet always respectful." Cooper was among seven soldiers killed Feb. 21 when a Blackhawk helicopter crashed during a medical evacuation mission in Saudi Arabia.

DALLAS RAY COOPER, 35
Army Staff Sgt.; Russellville, Mo.

The mechanic loved cowboy hats (with the brim pulled down) and 1,300-horsepower helicopter engines. "Even off-duty time, he was always concerned about the helicopter," said Warrant Officer George James. The gulf-bound father of two died Dec. 14 in a helicopter that crashed near Houston.

DALE THOMAS CORMIER, 30
Air Force Capt.; Crystal Lake, Ill.

Cormier wanted to make the Air Force his career; flying was his life. "I think of him as a real confident fighter pilot. He loved to fly," said his brother. Cormier died when his F-16 fighter crashed while returning from a combat mission.

ISMAEL COTTO, 27
Marine Cpl.; Bronx, N.Y.

The son of a Bronx factory worker, Cotto died in late January during the battle for Khafji. "We grew up poor, and we still are poor, and he didn't see things getting better," said his brother, Carlos. "He got fed up with the way things were for us, and he decided to join the Marines."

GARY W. CRASK, 21
Army Spec.; Cantrall, Ill.

Crask had served his three-year hitch and was 10 days away from discharge when the Army revoked his papers and sent him to Saudi Arabia.

He had joined the Army to travel and to create a future

or himself, but he had tired of the routine and wanted to et out, said his mother, Carolyn. He planned to study ngineering. A member of the 7th Engineer Brigade, he lied Jan. 17 when his sandbag bunker collapsed.

ALAN B. CRAVER, 32
Army Sgt.; Penn Hills, Pa.

His family called him "tough on the outside but soft n the inside." Craver, a reservist, was engaged to be married. He died Feb. 25 in a Scud missile attack.

JAMES CROCKFORD, 30,
Navy Petty Officer; Venice, Calif.

Crockford was a member of Helicopter Cargo Squadon 8, which ferried supplies, mail and people between hips. His helicopter developed mechanical problems Feb. 22 and crashed in the Red Sea.

WILLIAM D. CRONIN, JR., 29
Marine Capt.; Elmhurst, Ill.

He was one of eight Marines killed in a two-helicopter ollision in the Arabian Sea Oct. 7. He entered the Marines after graduating from Southern Illinois University a 1984. Earlier in the summer, he helped earthquake ictims in the Philippines. "He was doing what he oved," said his mother, Sheila.

DAVID R. "SKIPPER" CRUMBY, JR., 26
Army Sgt.; Long Beach, Calif.

Crumby was killed outside his armored car in a battle with the Republican Guard near the war's end. "I know it's selfish, but I wish it had been somebody else," said his mother, Annette.

JAMES B. CUNNINGHAM, 22
Marine Lance Cpl.; Glendale, Ariz.

Sleeping in his unit's tent camp in Saudi Arabia in November, he was killed by a bullet fired from another Marine's rifle. Officials ruled the shooting accidental. His mother said he "always loved sports and girls."

MICHAEL C. DAILEY, JR., 19
Army Pfc.; Klamath Falls, Ore.

Dailey loved salmon fishing on the Rogue River, said his father, Michael Dailey, Sr. "Every letter he has ever written asked about who was catching fish on the Rogue. I can hear him yell, 'Fish on!' "

A mortar man with the 3rd Armored Cavalry Regiment from Fort Bliss, Texas, Dailey died March 3 of injuries suffered March 2 when he apparently stepped on a land mine while on guard duty. He had enlisted at age 17, with his mother's permission. "When he called his mother from Saudi Arabia, she told him she wished she had never signed those papers," said Danell Dailey, Michael's wife, who eloped with him three days before he shipped out to Saudi Arabia.

ROY T. DAMIAN, JR., 21
Army Spec.; Toto, Guam

The oldest of four children, Damian was the leader. He'd wake the family at midnight to bake cookies. He loved to dance the cha-cha and make barbecued chicken and spare ribs for cookouts. "He was extremely handsome. Girls were calling all the time. He was a stud," said his sister, Marcia.

Damian passed the civil service exam but turned it down for adventure in the Army. He called home twice from the gulf but was cut off both times. "That hurts," Marcia said. On March 2, he was killed by a land mine.

MICHAEL D. DANIELS, 20
Army Spec.; Fort Leavenworth, Kan.

His honeymoon was interrupted for deployment to the Gulf last August. "They were high school sweethearts and really in love. Now all she does is cry. It's all so very sad," said Merienne Felder, stepgrandmother of his widow, Misty.

Daniels died when his OH-58 scout helicopter crashed during a combat mission. Before his death, he wrote that a priest had blessed his helicopter. Inside the cockpit, he kept a crucifix, a rosary and a bottle of holy water. "God will watch over me," he wrote his wife.

DONALD DANIELSON, 35
Army Sgt.; Newark, Ohio

The reservist died when he was pulled into a wate
pump at a desalination plant on Dec. 29. His age was no
available.

ROBERT L. DAUGHERTY, JR., 20
Army Pfc.; Hollywood, Fla.

Daugherty, who joined up just after his eighteent
birthday, was apprehensive but "proud to wear the uni
form of the U.S. Army," said his father, Robert, Sr. Th
younger Daugherty, a Bradley Fighting Vehicle mechan
ic, was killed by an explosive in Saudi Arabia.

MANUEL M. DAVILA, 22
Army Spec.; Gillette, Wyo.

Davila was killed in action in the Persian Gulf war, o
Feb. 27, just hours before the cease-fire was declared
Flags were flown at half-staff in his hometown. One of 1
children, he was married to Jennifer Scott, also of Gil
lette. He leaves by 3-year-old daughter, Nicole.

MARTY R. DAVIS, 19
Army Pfc.; Salina, Kan.

Davis was captain of the wrestling team, cornerbac
on the football team and a track star (22.4 seconds in th
200-yard dash; 21 feet, 7 inches in the long jump). Bu
most important were his buddies — a multicultural

group of athletes (two black, one Hispanic, one white). "The Awesome Foursome," they called themselves.

When Davis' parents transferred to an Army base in Texas, Davis moved into the home of his best friend, Dan Allen. Davis slept downstairs. Allen slept upstairs. They worked together at a McDonald's. They double-dated in Allen's souped-up 1978 Chevy Nova. Davis sent his best friend an Arabic soda pop can as a souvenir. He was killed by a hand grenade on Feb. 25.

"When I lost my mother my senior year, he was there for me," Allen said. "We were as close as two people could be. I feel everything I cared about has been taken away."

TATIANA KHAGHANI DEES, 34
Army Staff Sgt.; Congers, N.Y.

A native of Tehran, Iran, Dees was a military policewoman who drowned Jan. 7 in Dhahran. She died after stepping backward off a pier while avoiding moving military cargo, and was unable to swim because of her gear. Dees, who is survived by two children, served with the 92nd MP Company, 93rd MP Battalion, 14th MP Brigade, V Corps, based in Germany. She aspired to be a lawyer, pursuing her education while in the military.

ROLANDO A. DELAGNEAU, 30
Army Cpl.; Nicaragua

He died in the Scud missile attack Feb. 25.

DELWIN DELGADO, 26
Navy Petty Officer; Jacksonville, Fla.

Delgado and 20 other U.S. sailors died Dec. 22 when their ferry capsized while returning to the USS *Saratoga* after Christmas leave in Israel. Delgado was so attached to his family, he asked a buddy to check on his mother and younger sister whenever he shipped out.

LUIS R. DELGADO, 30
Army Sgt.; Laredo, Texas

On weekends, Luis Delgado could be found in the California sunshine playing with his dark gray 1987 Camaro Z-28. He'd spend hours washing, waxing, shining the tires and souping up the engine.

A native of Patillas, Puerto Rico, Delgado moved to Laredo as a child. "He made me laugh," said his wife Marisol. They met at a friend's wedding and quickly fell in love. He'd sing his favorite salsa songs in the shower although he didn't have much of a voice. The family stayed home nights at Ford Ord in California to watch their favorite comedies: "Married with Children," "In Living Color" and "The Cosby Show."

Delgado, a combat engineer, died Feb. 26 while trying to disarm a mine inside Kuwait.

His son, Luis R. Delgado, Jr., turns three in April. Manuel, a son from a previous marriage, is five. "As for me," his wife said, "my son is all I have left."

THOMAS M. DIFFENBAUGH, 34
Marine Warrant Officer; Bakersfield, Calif.

Diffenbaugh, who had two daughters, died Jan. 5 in a head-on truck collision. He was a construction officer.

GARY S. DILLON, 29
Marine Capt.; Concord, N.H.

A 1983 graduate of the University of New Hampshire and a lacrosse player, Dillon was a pilot assigned to helicopters aboard the USS *Okinawa*. He was one of eight Marines killed in a mid-air collision Oct. 7. Dillon was engaged to be married, but he wrote his father that he approved of his assignment in the Mideast. "That's what he was in the service for," said his father.

YOUNG M. DILLON, 27
Army Sgt.; Aurora, Colo.

When a superior suggested Dillon apply to West Point, he said no. He wanted to be in the field, not school. He liked being outside with the boys, hunting, fishing and hiking.

Dillon died Feb. 26 in a firefight with the Republican Guard. He was a forward artillery observer assigned to the 3rd Armored Division. His job: go to the front and pinpoint the location of enemy tanks.

Dillon was a native of Korea. He moved to the United States in grade school after his mother, Ok Hee Dillon, married Larry Dillon. He was a high school wrestler. In his senior year, he and his buddies tossed about ideas on what to do after school. They all joined the service.

He met his German wife, Cassie, while stationed in that country. A baby, Daniel, was born seven months before his father died. Cassie is pregnant again, expecting in July. She plans to visit Colorado for the burial at Fort Logan National Cemetery in Denver, then return to Hanau, Germany, to raise her children. "I hope to change her mind. I'd like her to stay," said Larry Dillon.

KEVIN R. DOLVIN, 29
Marine Capt.; Mineral City, Ohio

With his enlistment up next year, Dolvin was considering leaving the Marines in order to remain closer to his family. He was among eight killed in a helicopter collision Oct. 8 over the Arabian Sea. He had two sons, 4 years old and 9 months old.

DAVID Q. DOUTHIT, 24
Army Sgt.; Tacoma, Wash.

A crew chief on an armored personnel carrier, Douthit died Feb. 27, shortly before the cease-fire and a month before his first child was due to be born to his wife, Jessica. Douthit and Jessica met in Germany, where she was reared and he was stationed with the Army. "He wanted to go back to Alaska and fish and work on cars," said best friend Army Sgt. Steve Brown. "He loved to fish."

ROBERT J. DWYER, 32
Navy Lt.; Worthington, Ohio

Dwyer, a Navy F/A-18 pilot, was killed on a bombing mission.

JONATHAN "JACK" EDWARDS, 34
Marine Capt.; Grand Rapids, Mich.

Edwards, who died Feb. 2 when his Cobra helicopter crashed during a medical evacuation mission, was the first gulf casualty to be buried at Arlington National Cemetery.

PAUL R. EICHENLAUB II, 29
Air Force Capt.; Bentonville, Ark.

The grandson of a World War II pilot, Eichenlaub knew in kindergarten that he wanted to fly. The electronic-warfare officer died Feb. 14, after his radar-jamming plane crashed returning from a mission.

MARIO FAJARDO, 29
Army Capt.; Flushing, N.Y.

Fajardo's degree in electrical engineering prepared him for a lucrative career. But his goal was to make Army major, said his mother, Sonia Santiago. On Feb. 26, he was one of eight soldiers killed while dismantling a land mine. His mother was especially proud of her son because she said he proved that Ecuadoran immigrants can rise above menial jobs.

STEVE FARNEN, 22
Army Spec.; Salisbury, Mo.

He'd already pulled a hitch in the Army, was out, working in a store near his folks' home and taking flying lessons to become a commercial pilot. The day he was scheduled to start final training for his pilot's license, he was called up by his reserve unit and sent to the gulf. In less than a month, Feb. 25, Farnen was among those killed when an Iraqi Scud missile hit his barracks.

ELISEO FELIX, JR., 19
Marine Lance Cpl.; Avondale, Ariz.

St. John Vianney Church was packed with mourners at services for Felix, the former altar boy who died Feb. 2 in friendly fire.

DOUGLAS LANCE FIELDER, 22
Army Cpl.; Nashville, Tenn.

When Fielder learned he was being sent to the Persian Gulf from Germany, where he had been stationed with the 7th Engineering Brigade of the 82nd Airborne Division, he wrote his grandmother, Evelyn Drevenstedt. If he was killed, he wrote his beloved Memaw — who used to holler loudest at his Little League games — he wanted to be buried in his green fatigues for his military funeral.

Fielder died Feb. 26 during an exchange of small-arms fire.

MICHAEL LLOYD FITZ, 18
Army Pvt.; Horicon, Wis.

Fitz enlisted in the Army Aug. 29, three months after he graduated from Horicon High School. Although he had been assigned to Fort Hood, Texas, he never set foot on base. Instead, he completed basic training at Fort Dix, N.J., and advanced training at Aberdeen (Md.) Proving Grounds, went home for a week's leave, then immediately reported to Fort Benning, Ga., Feb. 14, to be shipped to Saudi Arabia. Two weeks later — Feb. 27, just hours before the cease-fire — he died in artillery fire.

ANTHONY J. FLEMING, 25
Navy Petty Officer; Ashtabula, Ohio

Fleming, a minister's son, broke his arm as a child while pretending to be Superman. He set the Ashtabula High School record in the 100-meter dash. He died Dec. 22 when a ferry capsized while taking him back to the USS *Saratoga* after Christmas leave in Israel.

GILBERT FONTAINE, 22
Navy Aviation Storekeeper; Spring Valley, N.Y.

Fontaine's dream of becoming a pilot was dashed when he was told his vision wasn't good enough. He still wanted to serve, so he enlisted in the Navy. He died when the ferry he was riding capsized Dec. 22 on his way back to the USS *Saratoga*. Fontaine's mother returned home from Christmas shopping to find three Navy officers who had waited four hours to give her the news of her son's death.

IRA FOREMAN, 30
Army Sgt.; Dayton, Ohio

His mother's statement, read at his funeral: "Ira never wanted anyone to worry about him." He died Feb. 17 when the military vehicle in which he was riding crashed and flipped over twice.

ARTHUR GALVAN, 33
Air Force Capt.; Navarre, Fla.

He was an enlisted airman who earned his commission through Troy State University's ROTC program. A "very methodical person," Galvan designed a wooden playhouse for son Jason – it resembles the family house and has electricity – on his computer. His wife, Suzanna, said, "He loved playing religious music and tunes from the '50s, '60s and '70s on his guitar." A fire control officer, Galvan was aboard a gunship that crashed Jan. 31. Listed as MIAs, all 14 crew members were believed to be dead.

SAMUEL GARDNER, 35
Air Force Master Sgt.; Idalou, Texas

Gardner packed his sand wedge so he could keep on top of his golf game in the desert. He was stationed at Hahn Air Force Base in Shoren, Germany, but was thinking of retiring to be closer to his family in Texas. He died in the August 28 plane crash in Germany.

MIKE ALAN GARRETT, 31
Army Staff Sgt; Laurel, Miss.

Patricia Garrett believes her son lived in the wrong century. "I have always said he should have been born 150 years ago because he loved that life out in the woods like our pioneers had," she said. "I remember one summer he didn't sleep in the house half a dozen times. He camped out in the pasture with his friends."

Garrett, a helicopter crew chief and mechanic, kept his mother's freezer well stocked with catfish, perch and bass. "He could put his line in a mud puddle and catch a fish," his mother recalled. Garrett, divorced since 1981, had one son, Shaun, 13. Garrett died in a helicopter accident while transporting Iraqi prisoners of war.

PHILLIP GARVEY, 39
Army Chief Warrant Officer; Pensacola, Fla.

The 22-year Army pilot and Vietnam vet didn't have to go to Saudi Arabia, but asked to go "because he didn't have small children at home, and he wanted to save someone else from having to leave their small children behind," said his sister.

On Feb. 27, he died after Iraqi anti-aircraft fire shot down his Blackhawk helicopter as it streaked to save a downed F-16 pilot.

"When the chips were down, you couldn't ask for a better friend," said high school buddy Ricky Sharpless.

ARTHUR O. GARZA, 20
Marine Lance Cpl.; Kingsville, Texas

Garza died the last week of January when his armored vehicle crashed.

DANIEL GARZA, 24
Air Force Staff Sgt.; San Antonio, Texas

Before getting his activation orders in August, the crew chief wore his flight suit and kept his packed luggage with him, said his mother. "He was happy the night before he left. He said he'd had a dream the week before that he was delivered to God." The reservist died in a late August crash of a C-5A transport plane in Germany.

KENNETH BLAINE GENTRY, 32
Army Sgt.; Ringgold, Va.

Gentry didn't enlist until he was 25, but all his childhood toys had been tanks and soldiers. He was stationed in Germany, where he lived with his wife, and son and daughter, when he was shipped out to Saudi Arabia Dec. 23.

A gunner with the 4th Squadron of the 7th Cavalry, Gentry died Feb. 26 when his armored vehicle struck a land mine. Gentry had been in the Army seven years. "He was thinking of making a career of it," said his father, Howard.

JOHN GILLESPIE, 34
Army Maj.; Bala-Cynwyd, Pa.

Soledad Gillespie's son was an overweight youngster who was called "dummy" by those unaware of the fact he had dyslexia, a learning disability. His sister, Cristina Hart, said he had had a stormy adolescence. But his uncle inspired him during his final year in high school. His grades improved, he graduated from Lincoln University, joined the Army and went to Michigan State, where he became an osteopathic physician. On duty in the Persian

Gulf with the 28th Medical Hospital, XVIIIth Airborne Corps; he died when the truck he was riding in flipped over. He'd been married only a little more than a year.

DAVID GILLILAND, 21
Navy Petty Officer; Rolla, Mo.

Gilliland, a boiler technician on the USS *Iwo Jima*, was killed Oct. 30 when a steam pipe burst. His father, Hank, said, "We just thank God we had a kid like him."

ROBERT G. GODFREY, 32
Army Chief Warrant Officer; Phenix City, Ala.

Godfrey grew up in Cedartown, Ga., and the Army seemed the best way out, his wife said. The smalltown boy went on to become one of the best chopper pilots in the service, said his commander at Fort Rucker, Ala. — "so good that he was instructor for other pilot instructors." On Feb. 27, Godfrey's Blackhawk was shot down by Iraqi anti-aircraft fire while on a rescue mission.

JOHN M. GORDON, 46
Air Force Maj.; Spring, Texas

He was commander of the C-5A cargo plane en route to the Persian Gulf when it crashed in late August shortly after takeoff in Germany. A Houston telecommunications executive and father of three, Gordon might not have been flying that night had he waited for his San Antonio–based reserve unit to be officially activated. But he had volunteered for early active duty. "He left on Aug. 8, and I never saw him again," said Judy Gordon, his wife of 23 years.

At Gordon's full military honors funeral, 800 friends

from all over the country attended. "John never met a stranger," said his wife.

DANIEL EUGENE GRAYBEAL, 25
Army 1st Lt.; Johnson City, Tenn.

Graybeal's ambulance helicopter, a UH-1H Huey with the 507th Medical Company, crashed Feb. 27 on a mission in the gulf. He graduated from East Tennessee State University in 1987.

TROY LORENZO GREGORY, 21
Marine Lance Cpl.; Richmond, Va.

Gregory was seriously wounded Feb. 27 and later died from injuries suffered after stepping on a land mine near a Kuwait oil field. His mother said, "This is about the hardest thing I've ever had to go through. It's a pain inside of me that I can't get rid of."

WILLIAM D. GRIMM, 28
Air Force Capt.; Hurlburt Field, Fla.

Listed as MIA, he was a crew member of an Air Force gunship that crashed Jan. 31. All crew members were believed to be dead.

ALBERT G. HADDAD, JR., 22
Marine Cpl.; Denton, Texas

His father, Lt. Col. Albert G. Haddad, piloted Air Force transports during the Vietnam War. And his sister is now serving in the military. "It must have been in the family," said Debbie Cross, a secretary at Lewisville High in Texas, where Haddad graduated as an honors student in 1986. "I can picture him in his football uniform. He was the type of person that you would like your own son to grow up to be like. He was a model student, very respectful, very courteous, just a good all-round student, and a gentleman."

Haddad, one of four Marines who died when their helicopter crashed Feb. 2, married his high school sweetheart, Cindy, five months before his death.

THOMAS J. HAGGERTY, 26
Army 1st Lt.; Marstons Mills, Mass.

His three-year commitment was up last October, but he extended it to serve in the gulf. Haggerty died while demonstrating the use of an automatic pistol. It accidentally fired, killing him. One of eight children, he was a Dean's List student at Norwich University in Vermont.

Joseph King, valedictorian of Haggerty's 1983 high school class, knew Haggerty since the second grade. "I remember his first day in school. He sat across from me, the new kid, a big baseball fan. Remember the movie *Stand by Me*? He was my best friend."

GARLAND V. HAILEY, 37
Army Staff Sgt.; Baltimore, Md.

Hailey, a medical evacuation specialist, died Jan. 19 when the UH-60 Blackhawk helicopter he was aboard crashed while evacuating injured soldiers. He had served two tours in Korea, and came to the gulf from Germany, where he lived with his Korean-born wife, Hye Cha, and his 5-year-old son.

TRACY HAMPTON, 26
Army Sgt.; Kirchgoens, Germany

Hampton, assigned to the 3rd Field Artillery, died Jan. 15 when his bunker collapsed.

JOE H. HANCOCK, 49
Army Lt. Col.; Nashville, Tenn.

Hancock, a distribution company marketing manager, was found dead Dec. 1 in his tent with a bullet in his temple. The military called it an apparent suicide, but his Congressman has called for an investigation. "Everybody who knows Joe cannot believe he would have done this to himself," said Jim Dyer, the brother-in-law of Hancock's widow, Sally.

STEVEN MARK HANSEN, 28
Army Staff Sgt.; Ludington, Mich.

An avid outdoorsman, Hansen especially enjoyed fishing and hunting deer and rabbits in Michigan's Upper Peninsula with his father and brother. His family spent a happy, quiet Christmas knowing he'd be leaving for Saudi Arabia Jan. 16. A trained engineer with nine years of service, Hansen died March 1 when he stepped on a land mine.

MICHAEL ANTHONY HARRIS, 26
Army Sgt.; Pollocksville, N.C.

As a child, Harris collected boxes and boxes of toy soldiers. Said his mother, Mabel: "You had to be careful not to knock them down." Harris joined the military in 1983, fresh out of high school. The Army was his life.

The single combat engineer, based out of Fort Bragg, arrived in Saudi Arabia in August. He was among the soldiers killed Feb. 26 while disarming a land mine at an Iraqi air field. "I had dreamed about Army people coming to tell me of his death," said his mother, "and wondered why I had this dream. You kind of dismiss it."

TIMOTHY R. HARRISON, 31
Air Force Staff Sgt.; Maxwell, Iowa

A gunner on an AC-130, the 12-year Air Force veteran was married to the military. "He wanted to fly ever since he was a kid," said sister Sandy Viers.

A happy-go-lucky middle child, Harrison adored cars, from the remote-control version to stock cars to everything in between. "Cars were his second wife," she said. Harrison was listed as MIA when his plane crashed Jan. 31. All 14 crew members are believed dead.

ADRIAN J. HART, 26
Army Spec.; Albuquerque, N.M.

Hart cared for his invalid mother. He was killed Feb. 8 in a truck accident in Saudi Arabia. He hadn't seen his father since he was age 4. He last spoke to him on the phone at age 18. "I never had a chance to get to know my son," said his father, Paul. "I had always thought we'd have time to fix things."

RAYMOND ELIJAH HATCHER, JR., 32
Army Staff Sgt.; Monticello, Fla.

Hatcher was "a big guy with a hot temper," said his sister. He put those qualities to use for the country by leading a platoon of 30 men into Kuwait days before he was killed March 2 in an accidental explosion. In a valentine to his wife, he called her "a pretty good woman for putting up with me." Hatcher's unit came back to the U.S.A. five days after his death.

JIMMY D. HAWS, 28
Army Sgt.; Traver, Calif.

His 3-year-old son, Roger Lee, "was the most important thing in the world to him," said his mother, Faye. Her son left school and joined the Army on his eighteenth birthday. The computer technician for anti-aircraft vehicles was on his third enlistment, after two tours in Germany. Haws was killed Feb. 20, when his anti-aircraft vehicle was hit.

JAMES D. HAWTHORNE, 24
Marine Sgt.; Stinnett, Texas

Training in an M1-A1 tank was a dream come true for Hawthorne. "You'd love them," he told his parents. "They're the greatest thing the military has ever come up with." A knee injury during training in California almost kept Hawthorne out of the gulf, but he recovered in time to get his wish: to be a Marine tank commander.

An avid hunter and fisherman, Hawthorne also had tried his hand at rodeo and boxing. But the Marines were No. 1, said his mother, Jerri. Hawthorne died in Kuwait February 27 when he was hit by shrapnel.

WADE E. HECTOR, 22
Army Spec.; Newport, N.H.

He loved the outdoors. For fun Hector would go dirt-biking, hiking, camping and hunting. On the shooting range, he loved to compete, winning high honors in the 1990 Shooting Competition with the Vermont Postal League. Death came in a non-combat truck accident Feb. 22. He was engaged to be married.

ERIC D. HEDEEN, 27
Air Force 1st Lt.; Malaga, Wash.

"Eric was an officer, but he was also my friend, my best friend and my husband," said Susan Brye-Hedeen. The son of a retired Air Force fighter pilot, Eric died Feb. 2 when the B-52 bomber he was aboard crashed into the Indian Ocean after a bombing mission.

KERRY P. HEIN, 28
Army Warrant Officer; Sound Beach, N.Y.

The medevac pilot died Feb. 27 when his Huey helicopter crashed. He arrived in Saudi Arabia on Christmas Eve with the 507th Medical Company.

BARRY HENDERSON, 40
Air Force Maj.; Tuscumbia, Ala.

A chemical engineer with the Tennessee Valley Authority, Henderson grew up dreaming of flying — even as a boy on an Alabama cotton farm. "If I could bring my brother back," said Lamar Henderson, "he would have wanted a chance to fly again."

Married and the father of two sons, he was killed when his Air Force RF-4C Phantom jet crashed in Saudi Arabia in October.

DAVID R. "CHIP" HERR, JR., 28
Marine Capt.; Fort Worth, Texas

A graduate of Washington and Lee University, he did crossword puzzles in ink, said his mother, Connie Herr.

After the Herrs were notified that their son was one of four Marines who died when the UH-1 utility helicopter he was co-piloting crashed Feb. 2, they took a walk and, said his mother, they decided there wasn't a single moment they would change about his growing up.

ROSENDO HERRERA, 45
Air Force Master Sgt.; San Antonio, Texas

The flight engineer died in the crash of a C-5A transport plane in Germany in late August. "He'd been on several missions before, and it was just something that he volunteered to do," said his son, Rosendo James.

DAVID L. HEYMAN, 28
Army Spec.; Hazelwood, Mo.

Heyman and his wife, Tabatha, had a baby in July. "He just beamed at that baby," said his mother, Jacquelin. When he last called, Heyman said he was safe, watching over generators. He and two others were killed when a plywood pallet fell on them on Feb. 28.

TIMOTHY HILL, 23
Army Spec.; Detroit, Mich.

Hill sorted toys to give children at Christmas and often set the table for the church coffee hour, recalled the pastor's wife at his church. A mechanic, Hill died Feb. 27 in ground fighting.

KEVIN J. HILLS, 19
Navy Electrician's Mate; Genoa, Ill.

His parents were home Christmas Day waiting for their only son to call. A Navy telegram arrived instead. The artistic young man had died Dec. 23, on his first shore leave, when a tour bus overturned. "Christmas, as we knew it is done," said his mother, Karen. "It will always be the time Kevin died."

ADAM T. HOAGE, 19
Marine Pfc.; Corona, Calif.

In one of his last letters, Hoage told girlfriend Kristie Angulo he wanted to marry her. Unsure of what career direction he should follow, Hoage joined the Marines after he graduated from high school. He was killed by a grenade explosion in a non-combat accident. Mellie Hoage, his mother, said, "I believe Adam was supposed to be where he was." Flags flew at half-staff at Norco High and Auburndale Junior High. "We were just all shaken up about it. Suddenly it all hit home," said the assistant principal.

ROBERT K. HODGES, 28
Air Force Tech. Sgt.; Hurlburt Field, Fla.

Listed as MIA, he was a crew member of the Air Force gunship that crashed Jan. 31. All crew members were believed to be dead.

LARRY HOGAN, 33
Marine Sgt.; Birmingham, Ala.

Based at Camp Lejeune, N.C., Hogan died of a gunshot wound Jan. 8.

DUANE W. HOLLEN, JR., 24
Army Spec.; Bellwood, Pa.

Hollen grew up in a central Pennsylvania valley, and it was on a nearby mountain that he was buried. He loved the mountains and the snow, said his wife, Wendy. The outdoorsman also enjoyed hunting game and tinkering with engines, trucks and cars. In late January, six months after being released from the Army, the reservist was called back to duty. He died when an Iraqi Scud missile hit his barracks in Saudi Arabia.

PETER S. HOOK, 36
Air Force Maj.; Bishop, Calif.

An Air Force Academy graduate and the son of a minister, Hook was killed when his F-15E Eagle crashed in the Persian Gulf Sept. 30. He was studying to be a Christian family counselor.

RAYMOND HORWATH, JR., 26
Marine Cpl.; Waukegan, Ill.

A combat engineer, Horwath died of an apparent heart attack aboard the USS *Shreveport* in the Persian Gulf Nov. 30. He graduated from Waukegan East High School in 1984 and joined the Marines two years later.

AARON W. HOWARD, 20
Army Pfc.; Battle Creek, Mich.

Howard's childhood dream of being in the Army faded quickly. After enlisting in 1989, he quickly became disillusioned and counted the days until his two-year tour of duty was up. His letters home from the gulf revealed fear and unhappiness.

In thanking a local Cub Scout den for a birthday present, Howard wrote: "There is no glory or glamor in war or being in the Army. Real life is not a *Rambo* movie, that's one thing I want you to understand. War is terrible and there are no such thing as heroes. All the heroes are dead and we don't need any more."

In his last letter to his mother, Bonnie Howard, he wrote, " 'Enjoy spring.' I frankly feel he had feelings of impending doom," she said.

Howard named the armored personnel carrier he drove Janis, after Janis Joplin. "I named her for the screaming wail of the engine and transmission while I'm driving," he wrote his mother. "I'm the pilot of the rolling coffin." Howard died Feb. 26 when his vehicle came under Iraqi artillery fire.

Howard requested that his body be cremated if he was killed. "He wanted us to scatter his ashes over a forest. He was very big into ecology and camping," said his mother, a funeral director. "I've planned over a thousand funerals. This is the hardest."

ROBERT HUGHES, 35
Army Chief Warrant Officer; Vernon, Conn.

The helicopter pilot "never wanted to shoot anyone," said his father, Richard. A 16-year Army veteran, Hughes died March 1 when the Chinook cargo helicopter he co-piloted crashed in a non-combat mission in Saudi

Arabia. In an upbeat note to his parents that arrived three days after his death, he praised Gen. Norman Schwarzkopf for his battle strategies.

RANDE HULEC, 29
Air Force Staff Sgt.; Cleveland, Ohio

Hulec, a marathon runner, was killed in late August in an Air Force C-5A transport crash in Ramstein, Germany. The nine-year Air Force veteran was a meteorologist stationed in Germany. He had been scheduled to take an earlier flight but it was full.

DANIEL V. HULL, 31
Navy Lt.; Chula Vista, Texas

A native of Dallas, Hull was commissioned an ensign when he graduated in 1981 from Texas A&M. He was lost at sea Dec. 19 when his Huey helicopter crashed into the Pacific Ocean, north of Guam, during a night training operation.

PATRICK R. HURLEY, 37
Army Sgt. Maj.; New Douglas, Ill.

A member of the U.S. Army Special Forces, Hurley was killed Feb. 20 when his helicopter crashed over Saudi Arabia.

An 18-year Army veteran who joined after graduating from high school, Hurley planned to retire in six months and hoped to study law, said longtime friend Jeff Rasnic.

A brother, Kevin Hurley of New Douglas, Ill., said Hurley had no reservations about taking part in Operation Desert Storm even though he was near retirement.

Hurley had been in the Persian Gulf for less than a

month before his death.

He is survived by his wife, Patricia, and three daughters, all of whom live at Fort Bragg.

WILLIAM J. HURLEY, 27
Marine Capt.; Chicago, Ill.

He used his ROTC scholarship to earn a degree in English from Marquette University. And once his commitment was up next December, said friends and relatives, Hurley might have left the Marines for a Peace Corps teaching job.

He died with seven others in an Oct. 8 collision of two helicopters over the Arabian Sea.

MARK HUTCHISON, 27
Navy Petty Officer; Elkins, W.Va.

He had been in the military since his high school graduation and served as a boiler technician. Hutchison and nine others were also killed in a boiler explosion aboard the USS *Iwo Jima* Oct. 30.

JOHN WESLEY HUTTO, 19
Army Pfc.; Andalusia, Ala.

Lil Lambert wrote a letter every day to her son after his deployment to the gulf in mid-August. The morning after the cease-fire, Lambert penned: "Well, I guess I won't be writing any more letters." Before she got the letter into an envelope, she learned of Hutto's death.

Her son's letters provided some comfort. Several arrived after his Feb. 27 combat death. One carried Lee Greenwood's lyrics to "God Bless the U.S.A."; another noted, "Hussein wants to pull out. We need to go ahead and roll him up so he won't come back in 5 to 15 years and start this all over again."

Lambert visited her son at Fort Stewart, Ga., shortly before deployment. Hutto hugged all the relatives before embracing his mother. He said "I saved the best for last."

WILTON L. HUYGHUE, JR., 20
Navy Fireman; St. Thomas, Virgin Islands

Huyghue was nicknamed "Pa" because, his mother explained, "When he was born, he looked like his great-grandpa." On the Saturday before Christmas his parents received a package of Christmas cards from him; only hours later, Navy officers arrived to inform them of his death. Huyghue was killed when the ferry he was riding in capsized as he returned from leave. Just before he died, Huyghue was notified he'd earned a promotion.

ARTHUR JACKSON, 36
Army Sgt.; Brent, Ala.

Four months short of his twentieth year in the Army, Jackson died in Saudi Arabia when a truck's brakes failed and he was caught beneath its rear tires.

KENNETH JACKSON, 22
Army Pfc.; Concord, N.C.

The last time he talked to his mother, Jackson asked for a tape of his 23-month-old daughter, Cherie, who had just begun to talk. The day before he died, he saw his cousin, Tracy Renee Carr, also in the gulf. He gave her a hat and two photos for Cherie. He died in Saudi Arabia Feb. 17 when his truck skidded out of control.

TIMOTHY JEROME JACKSON, 20
Navy Petty Officer; Anniston, Ala.

Jackson wanted to be an engineer and hoped the Navy would pay for his studies. "He liked to play his music loud. He liked to let you know he was coming," his mother said. He died Dec. 22 when his ferry capsized near Israel on the way back from Christmas leave.

JIMMY WESLEY JAMES, 22
Army Spec.; Willingboro, N.J.

James was frightened of going to the Persian Gulf. "Just close your eyes and Mom will be there," his mother, Maria, told him. But when James died Dec. 21 in a truck accident, his mother couldn't afford to fly to his funeral in Germany, where his wife of seven months wanted him buried. The Army refused to pay for her trip. "Don't let him be buried before I get there," his mother cried to a local newspaper. Neighbors raised $284. The American Red Cross picked up the rest of the cost. She made the trip.

THOMAS R. JARRELL, 20
Army Spec.; Alexander City, Ala.

Jarrell's mother, Tera Rice, remembered her son as a patriot. "When they were showing pictures on TV of flag burning, that just tore him up. He said, 'You don't do anything against the flag. You don't drop it on the ground, you don't let it touch the ground.' " Jarrell, a National Guardsman, was called up Nov. 18 and died March 3 when another soldier's weapon discharged accidentally.

THOMAS ALLEN JENKINS, 20
Marine Lance Cpl.; Mariposa, Calif.

"There are 500,000 people over there and this little community lost one right off the bat," said fellow volunteer firefighter Dan Marszalek, who fought his first fire alongside Jenkins. He died Jan. 20 in ground fighting.

DALE WILLIAM JOCK, 28
Navy Fireman Apprentice; Malone, N.Y.

A month before he died, Jock called his mother to ask for some of the things he left behind. Among the items was his high school yearbook. Jock, who joined the service two years ago, was scheduled to return home in February 1991. But on Sept. 11, aboard his command ship on duty in the gulf, the seaman suffered an apparent heart attack.

DANIEL D. JOEL, 23
Marine Cpl.; Glenbeulah, Wis.

His next of kin were told March 5 that he had died in a non-hostile incident. Further details weren't available.

ALEXANDER JONES, 19
Navy Airman Apprentice; St Louis, Mo.

Jones, a varsity baseball player, followed his 22-year-old brother into the Navy. The two boys and their five sisters were raised in a small house in the north St. Louis neighborhood of Walnut Park. His mother, Leola, called her son quiet and well behaved and said he was never tempted by the dangerous patterns of life in a poor neighborhood with few choices. Despite hating the water-

– and having never learned to swim – he joined the Navy right out of high school to learn a trade. Jones died in a ferry accident Dec. 22 returning from leave.

DANIEL M. JONES, 19
Navy Seaman; Wakefield, Mass.

An electrician's mate aboard USS *Antietam*, Jones was electrocuted Aug. 21 while working on the ship's ventilation system. Jones, who had five brothers and two sisters, joined the Navy, said a friend, because "he wanted money for college, to serve his country and, most of all, to have everybody be proud of him."

GLEN D. JONES, 21
Army Spec.; Grand Rapids, Minn.

He was discharged in July after a 31-month tour in Germany and was planning to attend art school to become a graphic artist. But he was reactivated when trouble started in the Persian Gulf. Jones arrived in Saudi Arabia on Feb. 16 and died nine days later when a Scud missile hit his barracks.

PHILLIP J. JONES, 21
Marine Cpl.; Atlanta, Ga.

"I couldn't read them at first," his mother said about two letters she received from her son after his death. "He asked about his [three] children and when was the last time I had seen them." Jones died of head injuries when a howitzer misfired Feb. 25. His mother said she battles "a hurt so deep I can't explain."

TROY JOSIAH, 25
Navy Petty Officer; St. Thomas, Virgin Islands

"Doc" Josiah and three other crewmen died Dec. 19 when their Navy helicopter crashed in the western Pacific Ocean during night training off the USS *Tripoli*. An avid swimmer, Josiah was a member of the military Search and Rescue team. He earned several awards playing flag football on the All Saints High School team.

JONATHAN H. KAMM, 25
Army Staff Sgt.; Mason, Ohio

A photo in his high school yearbook said it all: Above Kamm's head read "USA"; below, a takeoff on the Army slogan, "John Kamm is going to be all he can be." Indeed, he and his buddies talked a lot about signing up.

Kamm also liked to work on cars and spent three years in industrial technologies classes rebuilding cars. "I think we had about six Camaros," his teacher said.

On the day of the cease-fire, the seven-year veteran was helping transport troops in a Blackhawk helicopter behind enemy lines when it was shot down.

Kamm and his wife, Donna, would have celebrated their second wedding anniversary March 4. He leaves a son, Jeremy.

DAMON V. KANUHA, 28
Air Force Sgt.; San Diego, Calif.

Listed as MIA, he was a crew member of an Air Force gunship that crashed Jan. 31. The plane was located in waters off the coast of the Kuwait–Saudi Arabia border.

KENNETH T. KELLER, 26
Marine Sgt.; Glenville, Ill.

Since he was 18, Keller had been a Marine. He died Oct. 8, a few weeks short of his twenty-seventh birthday, when two helicopters collided over the Arabian Sea. He leaves a wife and son.

SHANNON PATRICK KELLEY, 23
Army 2nd Lt.; Gulf Breeze, Fla.

Kelley, a supply officer with the 101st Airborne Division, died Dec. 30 of a gunshot wound. Louis Sport, an ROTC buddy from University of West Florida, says, "I think he would have done everything he could to keep himself alive."

NATHANIEL H. KEMP, 18
Navy Spec. Apprentice; Greenwood, Fla.

Nicknamed "Bullet," Kemp played tuba and was a basketball center in high school. He was one of 21 sailors who drowned when their ferry sank returning from leave Dec. 22. Survivors include a 4-year-old brother.

FRANK S. KEOUGH, 22
Army Spec.; North Huntingdon, Pa.

The last time Keough saw his sister – she drove him to the base as his unit left – he didn't say much. "I'm sure he was scared," recalled Christine Poth. After four years of active duty, as a cook at Fort Hood, Texas, Keough was considering a career in business. He was killed in a Feb. 25 Scud missile attack.

ANTHONY W. KIDD, 21
Army Spec.; Lima, Ohio

Kidd was remembered by teachers at Lima High as a quiet, serious person who loved carpentry. He helped build two houses while he was a senior. He was killed March 1 when he stepped on a land mine.

JOHN R. KILKUS, 26
Marine Sgt.; Wakefield, Mass.

Before he even finished high school, Kilkus joined the Marines at 17. He earned his diploma while on active duty. During an October training mission in the Arabian Sea, Kilkus was killed with seven others when two helicopters crashed. "He loved what he was doing," said his wife, Laurie, a former Marine reservist.

JERRY LEON KING, 20
Army Pfc.; Winston-Salem, N.C.

Kenneth King said his son idolized the military way of life, fascinated with anything to do with a uniform. King, who was a twin, belonged to the high school Junior Reserve Officers' Training Corps and reported to Fort Bragg soon after graduating in 1989. Soldiers there nicknamed him "Purple" because almost everything he wore had "something with purple in it," said a close friend.

The combat engineer died Feb. 26 while clearing an Iraqi mine field. His father wonders what might have been: "It's like you drive down a road, take a fork and drive off a bridge. You wonder what would have happened if you had taken the other fork."

REUBEN G. KIRK III, 19
Army Pfc.; Dunlow, W.Va.

A high school football player and band member, Kirk died Jan. 29 in Saudi Arabia when a civilian tractor-trailer struck his Army truck. As a forward observer with the 1st Infantry Division, he searched out enemy targets and called in artillery strikes.

LONTY A. KNUTSON, 27
Air Force Tech. Sgt.; San Antonio, Texas

A reservist and a crew chief at Kelly Air Force Base, the father of two was killed in late August when his C-5A plane crashed in Germany.

DAVID W. KRAMER, 20
Army Pfc.; Palm Desert, Calif.

"He could have been anything he wanted," said the young soldier's father. Kramer had joined the Army to get money for college, and his dad had already mailed him college catalogs and newspaper ads for rental apartments. Then, in one of the last battles of the war, Kramer was killed in Kuwait when Iraqi fire hit his tank.

EDWIN BRIAN KUTZ, 26
Army Sgt.; Riverside, Calif.

Kutz mailed home a roll of film of him and his buddies in Saudi Arabia. The day his mother had it developed, she also learned of his death. The cavalry scout, who died Feb. 26 in combat, was buried in Kutztown, Pa., named after an ancestor. Survivors include his parents, a wife, two children and two stepchildren.

CHERYL LABEAU-O'BRIEN, 24
Army Sgt.; Racine, Wis.

LaBeau-O'Brien met her husband while serving in Germany. They were stationed together at Fort Riley, Kan., and their units worked closely in the gulf. The couple, a month shy of their first wedding anniversary when she died in a helicopter crash Feb. 27, saw each other for the last time two days before her death. "She came by to visit and give me a cassette with a song that she dedicated to us," Sgt. Michael J. O'Brien said. "The song was 'Without You' sung by Motley Crue. She gave me that tape and said, 'This is going to be our song.' "

VICTOR T. LAKE, JR., 22
Marine Cpl.; Jacksonville, N.C.

Lake, his brother and his brother-in-law, were all on active duty in the Persian Gulf. He died Feb. 27, when a grenade accidentally exploded.

DUSTIN C. LAMOUREAUX, 20
Army Pfc.; Bremerton, Wash.

"Dust" called home from Saudi Arabia at 2:30 a.m. Dec. 2. Lying in bed, his mother and father passed the phone back and forth for 45 minutes. "He was laughing and in great spirits," recalled his father, William. "Had we known the outcome, we would have woken his brothers." LaMoureaux was killed Dec. 5 after getting trapped between a truck and construction materials.

"My psychologist tells me I should keep writing him letters," said his father, a Vietnam veteran. "So I do. I write them, read them and file them away."

BRIAN L. LANE, 20
Marine Lance Cpl.; Bedford, Ind.

More than anything, Lane "loved to hunt," says his stepmother, Janice Lane. Lane died Feb. 26 during ground fighting at the Kuwait International Airport.

JAMES MICHAEL REYES LANG, 20
Marine Lance Cpl.; Oxon Hill, Md.

Lang was usually a quiet young man. But when he hit the road on a Friday night in his red Mitsubishi he cranked up the rock music "very loud," said his uncle Bob Lizama. The car, which Lang bought secondhand for $1,700 while he was training at Fort Detrick in Maryland, was the young Marine's passion. He put in a stereo system, covered the front bucket seats with sheepskin, installed louvers on the back window, and kept it shiny.

Lang, a Guam native, is believed to be the first Guamanian to die in the war. He was planning to study computer science or become a police officer. He was killed in Kuwait on March 1 when an explosive he was handling blew up.

RICHARD R. LEE, 36
Army Chief Warrant Officer; Wallingford, Conn.

Lee, killed in a helicopter crash in Saudi Arabia, was on his second tour of duty. His wife is an Army nurse.

RALPH E. LEWIS, 39
Army Staff Sgt.; Melbourne, Fla.

Lewis drowned in the Banana River Jan. 14, just

hours before his plane was to leave for the Persian Gulf. An Army intelligence specialist assigned to the J-STAR (Joint Surveillance and Target Radar System) at Patrick Air Force Base in Florida, he is survived by his wife and two daughters.

MICHAEL E. LINDERMAN, JR., 19
Marine Lance Cpl.; Roseburg, Ore.

The son of a career Navy man died Jan. 29 when a U.S. missile destroyed the armored vehicle in which he rode. "Mike had the philosophy that there was nothing he couldn't do," said his father.

J. SCOTT LINDSEY, 27
Army Cpl.; Springdale, Ark.

Lindsey was "an outdoor adventurist," said his father, retired Air Force Major Joe Lindsey. In a letter from the gulf, the father of three encouraged a niece to "hug a tree." Lindsey, who was with the 418th Infantry Battalion, 3rd Armored Division, was killed March 1 by flying shrapnel.

JAMES H. LOVE, 31
Navy Lt.; El Cajon, Calif.

"He loved the Navy, he loved flying and he felt strongly about their mission in the Gulf," said his wife, Cynthia.

Love taped several children's books for his three kids to listen to while he was gone. "It's his role as a daddy where he'll be missed most," said his wife. The helicopter pilot was killed in a crash Dec. 19.

JAMES H. LUMPKINS, 22
Marine Lance Cpl.; New Richmond, Ohio

His mother, Gloria Davis, "felt like ice water" when she heard that 11 Marines were killed in the fighting at Khafji Jan. 29, said Lumpkins' older sister, Carolyn Head. "She hasn't watched the news since."

DANIEL LUPATSKY, 22
Navy Petty Officer; Centralia, Pa.

Wed in Sept. 1989, Lupatsky spent most of his married life at sea. In his last letter home, he wrote, "So I just work, work, work to pass time and to keep my mind off the wife I had to leave behind." The electrician's mate was killed Oct. 30 in a boiler accident aboard the USS *Iwo Jima.*

ANTHONY MADISON, 27
Army Spec.; Monessen, Pa.

Madison's big desire was "to go into the military," remembered his football coach. After his Army hitch, he joined the reserves, promising his aunt, "Don't worry, I'll be back home." The father of two died when a Scud missile hit his barracks on Feb. 25.

GARY MAHAN, 23
Army Spec.; Bellmead, Texas

Mahan was ready to be discharged when he was assigned to the gulf. He died Jan. 1 when his vehicle collided with a tractor-trailer.

MICHAEL NUNNALLY MANNS, JR., 23
Navy Machinist's Mate; Bowling Green, Va.

Manns was among 10 sailors killed Oct. 30 in a boiler accident on the USS *Iwo Jima*. In his last conversation with his father, he talked about the tension of pending war. "He was enduring that with the rest of the boys, but he was not complaining," his father said.

STEVEN GLEN MASON, 23
Army Spec.; Paragould, Ark.

After his death, it was the little things his mother remembered. When Mason was 5 weeks old, "we took him down the river, showing him all the fishing spots," Peggye Hambrick said of her son, who remained an outdoorsman. He died in a Scud missile attack Feb. 25.

JAMES B. MAY II, 40
Air Force Master Sgt.; Fort Walton Beach, Fla.

Listed as MIA, he was a crew member of a gunship that crashed Jan. 31. All crewmen were believed to be dead.

CHRISTINE MAYES, 22
Army Spec.; Rochester Mills, Pa.

They were engaged the day she left for the gulf. Fiance David Fairbanks promised to hold the engagement ring for safekeeping until her return. "We hugged and kissed, and she went around the corner," he said. It was the last time he saw her. Mayes died when an Iraqi Scud missile leveled her barracks. "She didn't really want to be over there any more than the rest of them," he said. But, "that's what she got paid for, that's what she did."

EUGENE T. MCCARTHY, 35
Marine Maj.; Brooklyn, N.Y.

McCarthy, an undercover agent with the U.S. Drug Enforcement Administration, worked in Peru's Upper Huallaga Valley, a main source of the world's cocaine. A gung-ho guy, he'd go on raids and jump from helicopters. Then he was called up with the reserves. The son of a New York policeman, he died Feb. 3 when the helicopter he was piloting crashed on an escort mission in Saudi Arabia.

JAMES ROBERT MCCOY, 29
Army Cpl.; Wilmington, Del.

McCoy, the father of four, was in his second tour of duty when he died in combat Feb. 26. A music lover who used to sing in the bathtub, McCoy played trumpet in the high school band. Stationed in Germany, the mechanic was shipped to Saudi Arabia around Thanksgiving. "Tell everybody my unit is on the front line," the youngest of seven wrote his mother, "because we're the best there is."

BRENT A. MCCREIGHT, 23
Navy Airman; Eminence, Ky.

McCreight was known as a guy who planned ahead. The Navy aviation electrician had prepared for an expected Feb. 7 discharge with resumes ready to mail, a new truck stowed in his parents' garage. He and 20 sailors were killed returning from leave Dec. 22.

MELVIN D. MCDOUGLE, 35
Air Force Sgt.; Fayetteville, N.C.

When he left for the gulf, his mother cried for two weeks. "I just couldn't figure out why I was crying," she said. Her worst fears came true. On Dec. 20, a 105mm howitzer shell exploded during training, injuring McDougle. He died three days later.

CAROL L. MCKINNEY, 36
Army Chief Warrant Officer; Leslie, Mo.

The former phone operator joined the Army at age 29 and became a pilot. She was co-piloting an air ambulance Huey helicopter toward a ship in the Gulf of Mexico when her chopper crashed Dec. 14. She was the first woman to die in Operation Desert Shield.

McKinney left active duty in March 1990 and returned home to live with her mother, grow flowers and complete college. She continued flying in the National Guard. "I'm really going to miss that girl," said her mother, Erma. "She took care of me like I was her kid instead of the other way around."

DANIEL CLAYTON MCKINSEY, 21
Navy Fireman Apprentice; Hanover, Pa.

He made his first call home — and spoke with his mother and wife — the day before he died. McKinsey was one of 10 sailors killed in a boiler accident aboard the USS *Iwo Jima* Oct. 30. His wife, Kimberly, was expecting their first child in March. They found out she was pregnant the day before he got orders to go to Saudi Arabia as part of Operation Desert Shield.

BOBBY MCKNIGHT, 52
Army Spec.; Dallas, N.C.

Although McKnight was deacon of Mount Pisgah Baptist Church in Dallas, the funeral had to be moved to Friendship Baptist Church to hold the crowd of 500. He died in a vehicle accident Feb. 18 in Saudi Arabia.

JEFFREY MIDDLETON, 23
Army Cpl.; Oxford, Kan.

On Feb. 18, the couple's second anniversary, Gina heard that her husband the gunner in a Bradly fighting vehicle, had been killed by friendly fire the previous day. She wrote a special tribute for his memorial service: "He was kind, peaceful, sensitive, sincere and, above all, the most gentle person I have ever known. He loved thunderstorms, porch swings and video games. He valued family, country and love."

The Army was going to be Middleton's career. He'd just re-enlisted before the Persian Gulf crisis began. Oxford High School classmates, who set up a scholarship fund in his name, remembered him as a good friend.

JAMES ROBERT MILLER, JR., 20
Army Sgt.; Decatur, Ind.

Nearly six hours after the cease-fire began, he died after stepping on a land mine. Miller, who was a champion rifleman in high school, was delivering supplies to troops at the front. The Feb. 28 accident came a week after the birth of his second son. The family doesn't know if Miller received the telegram and photo of Matthew James, a name he helped pick out.

MARK A. MILLER, 20
Army Spec.; Cannelton, Ind.

Even as a child, Miller loved taking his Tonka toys apart. The mechanic died Feb. 25 in a non-combat situation about 20 miles south of the Iraqi border. "My son told me if he got killed in action, it would be an honorable death," said Charles Miller.

MICHAEL MILLS, 23
Army Spec.; Panora, Iowa

Called back to active duty after six years in the Army, Mills was in Saudi Arabia only six days when he was killed Feb. 22 by an Iraqi Scud missile. His wife expected their second child in April.

ADRIENNE L. MITCHELL, 20
Army Spec.; Moreno Valley, Calif.

"She just wanted to get out on her own — to finance her own education," said Mitchell's mother. Her father, retired from the Air Force, said, "I'm not a chauvinist, but I just don't think women belong in combat zones. I did 30 years, 21 days . . . and I didn't get a scratch. My daughter's been in for five months, and she's dead." She died in a Scud missile attack.

PHILLIP DEAN MOBLEY, 26
Army Cpl.; Blue Springs, Mo.

Mechanic Dean Mobley died in a land mine explosion March 1 — one day after his seven-year stint in the military was scheduled to end.

NELS ANDREW MOLLER, 23
Army Sgt.; Paul, Idaho

For the man believed to be the first Idahoan killed in the gulf war, peace came a little too late. Moller, an avid skiier and hunter, died Feb. 26 of injuries suffered in a tank battle with Iraqi forces. Said Idaho Sen. Steve Symms, a fraternity brother of Moller's father, "This really brings home the tragedy of war."

GARETT A. MONGRELLA, 25
Marine Sgt.; Hope Township, N.J.

Mongrella loved soccer and military history. He was killed, possibly by friendly fire, near Khafji Jan. 30. He left 18-month-old Anthony and his wife, Kim, a Navy veteran.

MICHAEL N. MONROE, 27
Marine Lt.; Auburn, Wash.

A musician and a triathlete, Monroe used his leaves to visit Asia, Australia and New Zealand. He was killed in a vehicle accident in October.

LANCE M. MONSEN, 35
Marine Staff Sgt.; Pembine, Wis.

Martha Monsen, a secretary at the U.S. Embassy in Bogota, Colombia, met her husband while he served as a Marine Corps guard there. "He was so handsome," she said. After a year off, Monsen made the Marines a career. "We had so many plans when he retired, but all that was turned upside down in one minute," she said. Monsen died of an apparent heart attack Jan. 10 in Saudi Arabia.

His wife and sons, Nicholas and Jonathan, are fulfilling one of Monsen's dreams — moving back to Wisconsin to live near his family. "The boys need a father figure."

CANDELARIO MONTALVO, 25
Marine Sgt.; Eagle Pass, Texas

Montalvo loved science and discovery, said his mother. He studied all the time, taking night classes near his base so he could become a chemical engineer. He joined the Marines seven years ago, after one year of college, because his family ran out of money. He had put the family first, said his mother. Don't worry, he told his father, "I'm going into the service and we'll be OK."

Montalvo married last August, but spent only three weeks with his wife. He never saw his first child, Brenda, born Jan. 31.

"I prayed and prayed that he would not be" called to the gulf, said his mother. "He told me, 'Mommy, please don't pray, I want to go to the war to see what a war is really like.' He was proud to be a Marine," she said.

On March 1, during clean-up operations in Kuwait, he died after a land mine exploded nearby. That same day, his mother received a letter he'd written. "I have found what fear is," it said in Spanish. "But I am not a coward."

THOMAS J. MORAN, 29
Marine Staff Sgt.; Cornwells Heights, Pa.

According to the Pentagon, the 12-year Marine veteran ended his life with a self-inflicted gunshot wound Sept. 26. He left behind a wife and two sons.

DONALD W. MORGAN, 30
Army Staff Sgt.; Ford, Va.

Donald and Ronald were twins. Ronald stayed home; Donald joined the Army. Morgan and best friend, Ricky Fulghum, followed each other on Army assignments around the world. Called "Donald Duck" as a kid, Morgan grew into a handsome man and was a meticulous dresser. He died Feb. 28 in a truck-loading accident.

JOHN K. MORGAN, 28
Army Warrant Officer; Bellevue, Wash.

"He had set as his goal to be a pilot, like his uncle," said his mother, Shirley Lansing. So after Morgan did a stint with the Navy, he enlisted in the Army. "When you're drawn to that, as my brother was, and he was a Vietnam fighter pilot, you don't count on getting shot down."

Morgan's family has created an aviation scholarship in his name at Puget Sound Bank, said his mother, that they plan "to give a young person who otherwise might not have the opportunity to fly."

JEFFREY F. MULLIN, 24
Army Sgt.; Weymouth, Mass.

Mullin, who was found dead of unknown causes in his tank on Jan. 14, never saw his daughter, Karla. His wife, Maria Guadaloupe, gave birth about three months after her husband, a member of the 3rd Armored Cavalry Regiment in Fort Bliss, Texas, was shipped out to the Persian Gulf.

JAMES MURRAY, JR., 20
Army Spec.; Conroe, Texas

As his wife, Katherine, rejoiced in the birth of their first child, officials arrived with the news that Murray had died. He was killed by a direct hit on the Bradley Fighting Vehicle he was driving in Iraq. On Feb. 26, Larissa Christine was born: 8 pounds, 3 ounces and 21 inches, with her father's round face and dark hair. Relatives are putting together a scrapbook of newspaper clippings and memorabilia from Murray's life for her.

DONALD R. MYERS, 29
Army Spec.; Paducah, Ky.

The Army was investigating the death of Myers, a radio operator with the 807th Medical Hospital, who was found dead in his sleeping bag March 2. His mother, Joanne, said she was told the Army was awaiting results of an autopsy.

JAMES F. NEBERMAN, 37
Civilian working for Army; DeWitt, Iowa

"See you when it's over," Neberman wrote to his brother in Wisconsin, where Neberman also grew up. The letter arrived two days after Neberman was killed, Feb. 25, when the vehicle he was driving in Saudi Arabia exploded. The defense department said he was the only civilian employee to die in the gulf war.

Neberman, survived by a wife, was "very easygoing, a little shy and reserved and intelligent," his brother said. "He was always trying to find the best in every situation," said Kristy Morrow, his sister-in-law.

RANDY L. NEEL, 19
Navy Airman Apprentice; Albuquerque, N.M.

Neel was photo editor of his high school yearbook and newspaper. He hoped to become a photojournalist. "The darkroom belonged to him. It was his second home," said yearbook adviser Leah Ready. He drowned Dec. 22 when his ferry capsized coming back from leave in Israel.

ROCKY J. NELSON, 21
Air Force Airman 1st Class; New Auburn, Wis.

Nelson had his own off-duty uniform: blue jeans, cowboy boots, T-shirt and a baseball cap. His favorite shirts were paper-thin and torn. "I'd throw them out; he'd retrieve them," said his wife, Cassie. In eighth grade, Nelson met Cassie: "He gave me a drink of pop at a football game." Her parents forbade dating because of their age, so they talked on the phone for hours. After graduation, Nelson joined the service. He wanted to get out early, but his wife talked him into staying so they could afford children. A daughter, Sasha, is 2. Nelson died Dec. 1 in a vehicle accident.

MICHAEL A. NOLINE, 20
Army Pfc.; San Carlos Indian Reservation, Ariz.

Noline's father, William, was refereeing a girls' basketball game on the Apache reservation when he heard his son had died. The tribal chairman announced at the game: "One of our Apache sons in the war has been killed. Stand up and pray." The father of two daughters, Noline died Jan. 26 when two trucks collided.

ROBERT A. NOONAN, 21
Army Spec.; Cincinnati, Ohio

The Noonans' family room doubles as a trophy room for the medals and certificates earned by Noonan, an anti-armor weapons specialist with the parachute infantry of the 82nd Airborne, said his father, a former paratrooper. He died Sept. 20 in a jeep accident.

JOHN L. OELSCHLAGER, 28
Air Force Staff Sgt.; Niceville, Fla.

Oelschlager loved the service. He was proud of his June promotion to technical sergeant. Oelschlager was on the gunship that crashed Jan. 31. Listed as MIAs, all 14 crew members were believed to be dead.

JEFFREY JON OLSON, 27
Air Force Capt.; Grand Forks, N.D.

An Air Force Academy graduate, Olson and his brother, Mark, followed in the footsteps of their father, Lt. Col. Norris Olson, a retired Air Force pilot. Olson died when his B-52 bomber went down in the Indian Ocean Feb. 2.

PATRICK B. OLSON, 25
Air Force 1st Lt.; Washington, N.C.

Since he was in the fifth grade, flying airplanes is "all he wanted to do," Daniel Olson said of his son who was shot down Feb. 27 returning from a combat mission.

PATBOUVIER E. ORTIZ, 27
Army Sgt.; Ridgewood, N.Y.

He was named after Patrick Bouvier Kennedy, President Kennedy's third child, who was born the same day but died shortly thereafter. "[It] was his father's idea," said Ortiz's mother, Hilda. "I tell you, he died hating that name." On Feb. 27, Iraqi anti-aircraft fire shot down his chopper. The next day, Hilda got a letter from him, along with a tape of him singing to her.

AARON A. PACK, 22
Marine Cpl.; Phoenix, Ariz.

"You can't prepare yourself for this," his father said. "Children are not made to die before their parents." Pack watched refugees streaming into Saudi Arabia and wrote "somebody has to help the little guys who can't help themselves." An artillery shell killed him in late February. He was with the 1st Marine Division.

WILLIAM FITZGERALD PALMER, 23
Army Cpl.; Hillsdale, Mich.

Elaine and Perry Palmer saw a transformation in their carefree, live-for-the-moment son who liked nothing better than to spin through the local gravel pits in his four-wheel-drive pickup.

His mother believes Palmer was a different man when he died Feb. 25. "He had really found himself there in the desert. With him being 23, he'd sowed a lot of wild oats. He didn't really worry about tomorrow. But he saw [in the gulf] that tomorrow was there waiting for him. We like to think he . . . died a man in the desert."

Knowing that, Elaine added, helped the family cope

with his death and rejoice when friends and family turned out for Hillsdale's biggest funeral ever.

FRED PARKER, JR., 24
Navy Petty Officer; Reidsville, N.C.

Parker, who grew up on a tobacco farm, originally was rejected by the military because he was overweight. So he lost 60 pounds. He traveled to France, Spain and Italy on shore leave. The boiler technician was killed in a boiler explosion Oct. 30 aboard the USS *Iwo Jima*.

DALE L. PAULSON, 36
Army Spec.; Sacramento, Calif.

Paulson, a communication systems operator, died Feb. 11 in Saudi Arabia in a non-hostile incident. Prior to his gulf deployment, he was assigned to the 93rd Signal Brigade in Germany.

DANIEL G. PEREZ, 50
Air Force Tech. Sgt.; San Antonio, Texas

One of 13 killed in the August crash in Germany of a gulf-bound transport plane, Perez left behind a wife and eight children. He and his wife, Olga, worked together at Kelly Air Force Base, where they met. Wed less than five years ago, the couple quickly had a full house. He brought five children from a previous marriage; she had three. He hated the word *step*. "To him, they were all his children," said his sister-in-law.

KENNETH JAMES PERRY, 23
Army Spec.; Lake Waccamaw, N.C.

Sonny Helms said his brother-in-law was a man with a sense of style and humor. And in that spirit Helms tells this story: A scholar and an athlete, Perry liked nice women, nice clothes and — especially — nice cars. One by one, however, he wrecked an MG sportscar, a Renault and a Monte Carlo — every car he ever owned.

"He just couldn't drive," chuckled Helms. "It was always funny that when he went into the service, they assigned him to drive the colonel around."

A chemical specialist, Perry died Feb. 25 in Kuwait when he was checking shrapnel for chemical residues and a bomb exploded.

"Kenneth was just so very unselfish. Every time he called from Saudi Arabia he was so worried about what it was going to cost us that he couldn't get in a good conversation," Helms said. "He thought it was going to be $35 or $40. I got the bill the other day and it was only $11."

DAVID G. PLASCH, 23
Army Warrant Officer; Portsmouth, N.H.

Plasch's pleasures in life were simple; he called his wife, Jana, seven times from overseas, often saying how he looked forward to raking leaves when he got home. When they finished their conversations, he'd get in line again to use the phone.

He got his pilot's license when he was 19 and flew small fixed-wing aircraft as a hobby. His mother said he was industrious as a child, cleaning up neighbors' yards for a quarter. He made the varsity soccer team in ninth grade when no one said he could. "He was ambitious," she recalled, "always trying to do things you had to be a lot older to do." His helicopter was shot down Feb. 27.

MARVIN J. PLUMMER, 27
Navy Boatswain's Mate; Ponte Vedra Beach, Fla.

Plummer drowned in a Dec. 22 ferry accident, a week before transferring to Italy. He leaves a son: Marvin II.

TERRY LAWRENCE PLUNK, 25
Army 1st Lt.; Vinton, Va.

News of Plunk's death ricocheted through the small town of Vinton, hours before the cease-fire was announced in the gulf. "It's tough on all of us. You could not find anybody in town who did not know what was going on," said Straley Pennington, a next-door neighbor who became something of a second father when his best friend — Plunk's father — died six years ago.

Plunk gave meaning to the cliche "All-American." Friends, neighbors, teachers remember him as a scholar, a jock, a strait-laced role model who sang tenor in the church choir, a popular guy who was the king of his high school prom, an outstanding soldier who was a star at Virginia Military Institute — the outstanding member of the senior class, by a vote of the faculty.

Said Pennington: "He had every reason to be arrogant with his accomplishments. But I never heard him."

A mine specialist, Plunk died Feb. 26 in Iraq while disarming explosives.

RAMONO LEVIAS POOLE, 21
Air Force Senior Airman; Sheffield, Ala.

Poole, who had a heart murmur and was being monitored for high blood pressure, was a surgical service specialist. Wanting to become a doctor, Poole re-enlisted a week before he died, Jan. 20, of an apparent heart attack. His wife, Tasha, also is in the Air Force.

CHRISTIAN J. PORTER, 20
Marine Lance Cpl.; Wood Dale, Ill.

Porter joined the Marines for the adventure, refusing his father's suggestion to try college first.

He loved basketball and basketball shoes, spending hours drawing new shoe designs on a computer. He talked about marketing his own designs one day. He died Feb. 27 during a tank battle between allied troops and an Iraqi Republican Guard division near the Kuwait City airport.

JAMES B. POULET, 34
Air Force Capt.; San Carlos, Calif.

Poulet was in college when he reluctantly strapped himself into a plane for the first time — for a flight to his summer job in Los Angeles. He came back saying flying was "the only way to go," recalled his father, Marcel. Once, Poulet tried to assuage his mother's fears about his passion for the cockpit: "Mom, if I die I'll die a happy man doing what I love to do." He died Sept. 30 when his F-15 fighter crashed over Saudi Arabia during a routine mission.

DODGE RANDELL POWELL, 28
Army Sgt.; Hollywood, Fla.

In a letter to his sister dated Jan. 25, Powell wrote that he had a "very good chance to die" because his unit would be near the front line. A member of the 82nd Engineer Battalion, Powell died Feb. 27.

RICHARD M. PRICE, 38
Air Force Reserve Maj.; San Antonio, Texas

He was the pilot of a gulf-bound C-5A cargo plane that crashed in Germany in late August. The night of the crash was their tenth wedding anniversary, said his widow, Susan. "After the funeral I got letters from around the world from people saying how he had touched their lives. A lot of the people he had only met once, but somehow they remembered him."

RONALD M. RANDAZZO, 24
Army Sgt.; Glen Burnie, Md.

His best friend remembered one fishing trip when they caught 200 fish. At Randazzo's funeral, a display of flowers was shaped like a fish, with a card: "I'll watch the fishing hole here, you watch the fishing hole there." He was killed with two others when their anti-aircraft vehicle was hit Feb. 20 by Iraqi fire.

Randazzo was a "well-mannered, well-motivated soldier" who wanted a career in law enforcement, probably the FBI, said 1st Sgt. Frank Schultz, who helped recruit his father and two of Randazzo's brothers (there were five boys) into the National Guard.

JEFFREY D. REEL, 21
Army Pfc.; Vincennes, Ind.

"I was lucky I got to talk to him before it happened. It was a fluke," said David Reel, who had spoken to his son just 16 hours before his death. Reel, whose term of duty in the Army was to end in March, was killed in February when the truck he was in overturned during military maneuvers. Reel joined the Army four years ago to take advantage of the scholarship program in preparation for college.

HAL H. REICHLE, 27
Army Chief Warrant Officer; Marietta, Ga.

He loved flying helicopters and hoped to turn his military talent into a peacetime career in the movies. Reichle formed a production company after serving as "aerial advisor" for *Firebirds* — a 1990 movie about the Army's elite helicopter task force, starring Nicholas Cage. A friend, John Brindo III, said Reichle wanted to do more of such work.

"I never met a more loyal, caring person in my life," Brindo told *The* [Cleveland] *Plain Dealer*. "He was a person who was not afraid to show how he felt. He always hugged me when he left. He was just one of a kind."

A former volunteer firefighter and police dispatcher, he served in the Marines, then switched to the Army because it offered him a chance to fly. He died in a helicopter crash Feb. 21.

FREDERICK A. REID, 33
Air Force Capt.; Harrisburg, Pa.

Reid never saw his second son, Cody. The birth came four weeks after Reid was sent to Saudi Arabia from England, where he had been stationed. He died Oct. 8 when his F-111 crashed during a training mission.

RONALD D. RENNISON, 21
Army Spec.; Dubuque, Iowa

Of her 27 grandchildren, he was one of Hazel's favorites. "My special one," she called him. "I favored him up." The oldest of three boys (one died as a child), Rennison and his dad both went to the gulf. The younger Rennison, nicknamed 'Tiger' because he made claws with his hands as a baby, was in the gulf a week before he was killed in the Feb. 25 Scud missile attack. Only a month earlier, he'd started a new job as a packer.

TODD C. RITCH, 20
Army Pfc.; Charlestown, N.H.

Ritch had pulled several men from a burning truck, saving their lives just prior to his death in a non-combat truck accident. He was a volunteer fireman, and his family asked that donations be made toward the purchase of a fire truck. According to his brother, Todd's wedding was put off, pending his return from the gulf.

MANUEL RIVERA, JR., 31
Marine Capt.; Bronx, N.Y.

A member of a Marine Attack Squadron, Rivera died when his F-4G jet crashed in a training accident in the Persian Gulf. New York City Mayor David Dinkins was among the more than 1,000 mourners at his funeral.

ERNEST RIVERS, 26
Marine Sgt.; Anderson, S.C.

Rivers, a former "A" student and football player, died Dec. 9 of a heart attack while taking an afternoon jog in the desert. Just before he died, he signed up for another six years. The seventh of 10 children, Rivers was the son of a sewing machine operator in a textile factory. "He didn't have a middle name. I had so many children," said Louise, his mother. Six of her children served in the military. In a phone call shortly before his death, Rivers made one request of his mother: send cookies.

MICHAEL R. ROBSON, 30
Army Staff Sgt.; Seminole, Fla.

Gen. Norman Schwarzkopf, at his briefing Feb. 28, described the heroism of a helicopter crew that crashed while rescuing a downed pilot who had broken his leg. Robson, a medic, was on that helicopter. The father of four boys — ages 1, 3, 9 and 12 — called his mother Feb. 11 so she could sing "Happy Birthday" to him.

ELOY A. RODRIGUEZ, JR., 34
Army Master Sgt.; Key West, Fla.

Before leaving for Saudi Arabia, Rodriguez told his family that if he died, he didn't want a military burial. The Rodriguez family has lived in Key West for 117 years, and Rodriguez, like his grandfather, wanted to be cremated and have his ashes scattered from a plane around the Florida Keys. Rodriguez was serving as a medic when he died in a helicopter crash Feb. 21 during a medical evacuation mission.

As a child, Rodriguez loved two things — flying and helping people. He graduated from Key West High School and, after one year at the University of Florida, enlisted in the Army. "We realized he was spending lunch money so he could jump out of planes," recalled his mother, Marlene. His last letter to his mother said:

"Remember, I believe in what I'm doing here, and it's my job." He left behind three children.

JEFFREY A. ROLLINS, 23
Army Sgt.; Bountiful, Utah

As a member of the 82nd Airborne, he loved to jump and was tickled to be selected. "He had a job and mission to do, and he was doing it," remembered his father, Robert, a Vietnam veteran. Rollins died Feb. 16 when his truck overturned in Saudi Arabia. He leaves a wife and 1-year-old son. He was a supply sergeant with the 307th Medical Battalion and had been accepted to train with the elite Golden Knights parachuting team.

TIMOTHY W. ROMEI, 22
Marine Cpl.; Alameda, Calif.

"He had maxed out his credit cards buying Christmas presents for us in Hong Kong in August, and he'd already shipped them home," said his mother, Tina Reber. A crew chief at Camp Pendleton's Marine Medium Helicopter Squadron 164, Romei died in a helicopter collision Oct. 8.

PETER J. ROSE, 26
Army 1st Lt.; Lincoln, Neb.

On Nov. 28, Rose said he was prepared to fight. "My mom doesn't like it. I mean, whose mom does? It's just something that happens." On Dec. 14, the helicopter pilot crashed near Houston on his way to Saudi Arabia.

MARIE T. ROSSI, 32
Army Maj.; Oradell, N.J.

She was one of the first pilots to fly into Iraqi territory, piloting a big cargo-carrying Chinook helicopter. To many, she exemplified the expanded role women played in the U.S. military. But Rossi downplayed this image: "What I am doing is no greater or no less than the man who is flying next to me. Or in back of me." Rossi died early this year when her helicopter hit an unlighted tower in northern Saudi Arabia during bad weather.

In an interview just prior to the ground offensive, she said, "Personally, as an aviator and a soldier, this is the moment that everybody trains for — that I've trained for — so I feel ready to meet a challenge."

Her husband, Chief Warrant Officer John A. Cayton, also a pilot, served in the gulf about 300 miles from his wife.

SCOTT A. RUSH, 19
Army Pfc.; Blaine, Minn.

Rush, a member of the 7th Engineer Brigade, died Jan. 17 when his sandbag bunker collapsed. "It is a weird feeling," he wrote a friend from the gulf, "looking around at friends and just people I know, wondering who is going to die, hoping it is not you, then again hoping it is you rather than a good friend."

LEONARD A. RUSS, 26
Army Sgt.; Pleasantville, N.J.

Russ planned to open a plumbing business and wanted to run for mayor of Pleasantville someday. He died in surgery in February after he was wounded by a gun that accidentally discharged. His brother, David, joined the Marines last May and graduated from boot camp 10 days before the funeral. At the funeral the Rev. Horace E. Burton said "his life was not lived in vain."

HENRY J. SANDERS, JR., 42
Army 1st Sgt.; Cocoa, Fla.

When death came in a vehicle accident Feb. 19, his sister remembered "a very quiet, very humble, very gentle person. His first love was baseball, but he loved to watch football, too." His mother, Louise, drew on her religion to stay strong: "Henry was a good boy. I don't have any hostility, because I study the word of God. I know He'll take care of us in good times and bad."

BALDWIN SATCHEL, 31
Army Sgt.; Courtland, Ala.

Satchel's brother, Charles, removed a yellow ribbon from his car at the funeral. "I said I wouldn't take it off until he came back. He's home now." Satchel died of an apparent heart attack Jan. 24.

MATTHEW J. SCHIEDLER, 20
Navy Boiler Tech.; Hubbard, Ore.

Schiedler wanted to enroll in the Naval Academy. He dreamed of being a pilot, although "he got sick on carnival rides," said his mother, Mary Ellen. He drowned when a ferry capsized Dec. 22 near Israel. "We thought on an aircraft carrier he was safe," said his father, George.

MARK SCHMAUSS, 30
Air Force Staff Sgt.; Hurlburt Field, Fla.

Schmauss was aboard an Air Force AC-130 gunship that crashed Jan. 31. Listed as MIAs, all 14 crew members were believed to be dead.

STEPHEN SCHRAMM, 43
Air Force Lt. Col.; Birmingham, Ala.

Schramm held the rank of major when his 117th Tactical Reconnaissance Wing of the Alabama Air National Guard was called up last August. He died during an Oct. 8 training crash and was promoted posthumously to lieutenant colonel.

SCOTT A. SCHROEDER, 20
Marine Pfc.; Wauwatosa, Wis.

A letter from Schroeder was posted in his brother Tad's seventh-grade classroom: "We're here to stop whatever Mr. Hussein wants to throw at us." He was killed Jan. 30, apparently by U.S. artillery fire, near Khafji.

BRADLEY SCHULDT, 27
Air Force Capt.; Arlington Heights, Ill.

"If Brad would have known what his death meant — as far as making a statement for God, for family, for country — he probably would have volunteered," his mother said. Schuldt packed 10 Bibles he intended to share with others in Saudi Arabia. He was stationed in Germany and died in late August when his C-5A cargo plane crashed en route to the gulf, where he was going to publish a newspaper for the troops.

BRIAN P. SCOTT, 22
Army Sgt.; Park Falls, Wis.

Brenda Scott lost her best friend and lifelong protector when her older — and only — brother died. "No one could touch his little sister," Brenda said. "When I was a freshman [in high school] he was a senior and he always had to approve of my boyfriends."

It went back even further than that. "We had a dog that was our other best friend when we were little so it was always the three of us," she recalled. "I remember one time the dog bit me in the ear and, because Brian was protecting me, he bit the dog back on his ear."

Brenda can't remember a time when her brother wasn't trying to fuss over her or someone else. It continued until the day he died. "When I talked to him he said, 'I'm not worried about me. I'm worried about my men,' " she said.

Scott's death carried an added note of tragedy: He had married the day before he left for the gulf and died without knowing about his son's birth. Casey Patrick was born two days before his father's Feb. 26 combat death.

TIMOTHY B. SEAY, 22
Navy Disbursing Clerk; Thomaston, Ga.

Seay is remembered as a popular teenager who was a member of the Navy Junior ROTC and senior class president. He drowned Dec. 22 when a ferry returning sailors from shore leave capsized in the Mediterranean Sea.

Seay had called home the day before and talked excitedly with his girlfriend and family about his newborn son, Timothy Jr., born Oct. 29. "He had just gotten the [baby] pictures, and he thought it was the best thing in the world," said his brother, Tommy.

JEFFREY A. SETTIMI, 25
Navy Seaman; Fort Wayne, Ind.

Cooking was one of Settimi's favorite pastimes, so he was well suited to his job as a baker aboard the USS *Saratoga*, said his aunt, Gina Settimi. "He said he wanted to have his own restaurant one day." His enlistment time was up in February, but he died Dec. 22 when his ferry capsized while bringing him back from leave. At his funeral, longtime friend Dann Zehr sang an original song that ended with the lines: "Your life was still worth living, Though shortened in the end, For lives like mine were better, Just knowing you, good friend."

DAVID A. SHAW, 33
Marine Staff Sgt.; Harrisville, Mich.

He wanted to be "just like his dad," a career Marine who had seen action in both Korea and Vietnam. He was serving as an assault amphibian crewman with the 1st Marine Division when he died of a heart attack Feb. 23. "He's always been quite lucky," said his father, James Shaw. "I thought he would come through without a scratch."

TIMOTHY ALAN SHAW, 21
Army Pfc.; Alexandria, Va.

"My baby led a good life," said Annette Brown of her only child. "He loved gospel music, he went to church. He was always helping people." Shaw worked for a telecommunications firm by day. At night, he was studying for a community college business degree. He arrived in Saudi Arabia on Feb. 19. Six days later, he was in an Army barracks that was leveled by a Scud missile.

EDWARD E. SHEFFIELD, 28
Air Force Staff Sgt.; San Antonio, Texas

A reservist, Sheffield worked for the city recreation department. He and his wife, Veronica, would walk and jog with the baby stroller after their daughter was born two years ago. In four years of active duty and three years of reserves, Sheffield never discussed not coming back from a mission. "I was trying to not think about it," said his wife, "so I could go on." Sheffield was a loadmaster aboard the gulf-bound C-5A cargo plane that crashed in Germany in late August.

JEFFREY SHUKERS, 28
Navy Chief Fire Control; Union, Iowa

Shukers was a romantic. When home, he'd bring his wife roses every week. Halfway around the world on her birthday last October, he made a long-distance radio dedication to her of Alabama's "When We Make Love."
He drowned Dec. 22 when a ferry capsized while

bringing sailors back from leave. Lori Shukers said her husband had looked forward to coming home and spending time with her and their son, Paul, almost 1.

STEPHEN J. SIKO, 24
Army Spec.; Latrobe, Pa.

Julius "Jute" Siko said the toughest moment wasn't hearing of his son's death in a February Scud missile attack. It was when he had to explain the death to his 5-year-old grandson. "I was telling him how his daddy got killed and went to heaven," the elder Siko said. "We were riding along and Jake just said to me, 'I want to die with my toys so I can play with my daddy in heaven.' And, boy, I'll tell you, I could hardly drive the car."

BRIAN K. SIMPSON, 22
Army Cpl.; Indianapolis, Ind.

Simpson and his 19-year-old wife were shopping for their first home when he was recalled to the military because of his specialty. A member of the 475th Quartermaster Group based at Fort Lee, Va., Simpson was a petroleum supply specialist. "He really didn't want to go, but of course he couldn't turn down his obligation," said his stepfather, James Jensen. Simpson was killed Feb. 25 in a Scud missile attack.

JAMES SMITH, JR., 22
Navy Petty Officer; Somerville, Tenn.

Smith was one of 10 sailors who died in a boiler explosion Oct. 30 aboard the USS *Iwo Jima.* He was captain of the 1986 Fayetteville-Ware High School basketball team. He is survived by a daughter.

RUSSELL G. SMITH, JR., 44
Army Sgt.; Fayetteville, N.C.

One day Pat Smith learned the war had taken her husband. Seventeen hours later a fire destroyed their rural North Carolina home. Smith, who had served in the Army for 17 years as an engineer and paratrooper, died Feb. 26 when a mine exploded.

DAVID T. SNYDER, 21
Marine Lance Cpl.; Kenmore, N.Y.

On Jan. 29, Snyder, who manned an anti-tank missile system atop a light-armored vehicle, died during an attack near the Saudi border. His parents were not bitter about military reports that their son may have been killed by allied gunfire. "He was just an average American kid," said his mother, Theresa. "He wasn't a great athlete, but if heart counted for anything, he would have been the all-star."

JOHN SNYDER, 25
Navy Lt.; Milltown, N.J.

"Almost from the beginning," Snyder knew he would join the armed forces, recalled a teacher. He set track records and made the honor roll at Spotswood High School. Snyder worked as the main propulsion assistant in charge of the steam engineering plant on the USS *Iwo Jima.* He died Oct. 30 in a steam accident aboard the ship.

BRIAN SPACKMAN, 22
Army Sgt.; Niles, Ohio

Spackman collapsed and died during a morning training session at Fort Bragg, N.C., on Jan. 14. He had celebrated a birthday the day before. A University of Akron senior and member of the 324th Military Police Company in Austintown, his first loves were archery and karate, in which he earned a black belt. "He was the kind of person who had a laid-back attitude, but when he had to get down to it, he could be aggressive," said his brother.

JEFFREY SPEICHER, 20
Army Pfc.; Camp Hill, Pa.

Speicher ran a photo lab for mapmaking in the back of a tractor-trailer. The truck jackknifed in a sandstorm Dec. 22, and he died Jan. 4 while undergoing plastic surgery in Germany. His fiancee, Mabel Rollins, whom he had postponed marrying until he returned from the gulf, was ready to board a plane for Germany just hours before he died.

CHRISTOPHER H. STEPHENS, 27
Army Staff Sgt.; Houston, Texas

He was one of four brothers stationed in the Persian Gulf. A preacher's son, Stephens died in Kuwait when Iraqi fire hit his tank Feb. 26. The Sunday after Stephens' death, his father — the Rev. Willie Stephens- — preached about pain to his Shady Missionary Baptist Church. The three brothers returned from the gulf to carry Stephens' coffin in his funeral.

DION J. STEPHENSON, 22
Marine Pfc.; Bountiful, Utah

Stephenson's idea of having fun was to jump off an 80-foot cliff into a lake. He dreamed of becoming a Hollywood stunt man. "He was a very gung-ho, no-challenge-too-big type of individual," said his father, James. His hero was actor Arnold Schwarzenegger, who used to work out with Stephenson's dad at a Las Vegas gym. Stephenson, a scout with a light armored vehicle, carried Schwarzenegger's picture to the gulf. When he died Feb. 29, fighting an Iraqi convoy, Schwarzenegger sent flowers and a telegram. Said James: "He wrote, 'To Dion, a true American hero, with love from Arnold.' It would have made his day."

ANTHONY STEWART, 19
Marine Lance Cpl.; Yonkers, N.Y.

Stewart, nicknamed "Pooh," hoped to escape his violent neighborhood. But on Dec. 29, he was accidentally shot in the head. Stewart was sitting on his cot, cleaning his weapon, when Lance Cpl. Steven Quiles' M-16 went off, according to a military report obtained by *New York Newsday*. "It was a mistake. I've killed a homeboy," said Quiles, of New York City. Quiles was sentenced to 15 months of hard labor for negligent homicide.

RODERICK T. STEWART, 20
Navy Petty Officer; Shreveport, La.

Stewart, an only child nicknamed "Ruka," called from Israel the day before he died. "He was excited because he wanted to see the Holy Land," said his mother. The former high school quarterback drowned Dec. 22 when his ferry capsized while returning from Israel.

ADRIAN L. STOKES, 20
Army Pfc.; Riverside, Calif.

"He loved the singing, he loved the camaraderie. He was a good basic kind of kid who found his niche in this singing group," said Ramona High School choir teacher Rick Woodbury, who had Stokes in his groups for six years. "At the end of the year, we go to Lake Paris, rent a pontoon boat and have a barbecue." Last year, a year after he graduated, Stokes showed up at the picnic. Woodbury said he teased him, telling him he was crashing a private party. "Come on, Woody," he remembers Stokes saying, "let us stay." He did, and a day later Stokes left for his Army basic training. He died Feb. 26 in combat.

THOMAS G. STONE, 20
Army Spec.; Falconer, N.Y.

With training from the Army, Stone thought he could build "a better future for us, for our daughter," said his wife. Instead, Stone was killed in a Scud missile attack. Before he died, he asked his family to send him a tape of Lee Greenwood's "God Bless the U.S.A."

GARY E. STREETER, 39
Army Sgt. 1st Class; Manhattan, Kan.

A 20-year career soldier decorated three times, Streeter was due to retire from the Army last Dec. 7. Instead, he was shipped from Fort Riley to Saudi Arabia.

His helicopter was shot down Feb. 27.

He and wife, Rose, had bought a house in Kansas in anticipation of his retirement, and after two tours of duty in Germany — one in Korea and one in Vietnam, Rose said, "We were going to take it easy."

The Persian Gulf war was harder to cope with than Vietnam, Streeter's wife said, "because for one thing we were younger and we hadn't had that much time together. Now we'd had 19 years together and we'd built a life."

WILLIAM A. STREHLOW, 27
Army Sgt.; Kenosha, Wis.

A seven-year Army veteran who wanted a military career, Strehlow leaves a wife, three small children and a sprawling — and patriotic — extended family in Kenosha. Strehlow died with two of his buddies in southern Iraq on Feb. 25 when they apparently were dismantling a bomb at a captured enemy air base. "He knew what he was up against," although he expressed frustration over being involved in a war over oil, said his mother, Cora. "But he said he knew he had his job to do and would do it."

PETER L. SWANO, JR., 20
Army Spec.; Salem, N.Y.

An intensely private young man, Swano never was photographed for his high school yearbook. However, when asked what his pet peeve was, he said "war." A member of the Headquarters Company of the 5th Cavalry, Swano died of an apparent heart attack Feb. 1.

GEORGE R. SWARTZENDRUBER, 24
Army Warrant Officer; Newton, Kan.

Swartzendruber, killed Feb. 27 when his Blackhawk helicopter was shot down, always loved flying. "George was reserved and quiet as far as talking — unless it came to airplanes," said his mother, Naomi. "Then he could talk all day."

Born in Kansas, Swartzendruber lived several places while his parents did missionary work. He graduated from high school in Papua, New Guinea. "He always had in back of his mind being a missionary pilot," said his father.

Swartzendruber, who died two days before his twenty-fifth birthday, loved restoring classic cars; his favorite was a 1962 Buick Skylark convertible.

JAMES H. SYLVIA, 23
Marine Cpl.; Putnam, Conn.

Sylvia loved baseball and scored the winning run when his high school team won the Connecticut state championship in 1985. A radio operator, Sylvia had called home two hours before he died Feb. 5 in a desert truck accident.

ROBERT D. TALLEY, 18
Army Pvt.; Newark, N.J.

Talley wasn't one of the "weeds" who turned to drugs or crime, the Rev. Jesse Jackson said at his funeral. He was one of the "tulips, the roses" who did well in high school and joined the military to achieve his dreams. Talley was killed by friendly fire in his Bradley Fighting Vehicle.

DAVID L. TAPLEY, 38
Army Sgt. 1st Class; Atwater, Calif.

Tapley, who was preparing to retire in 1992, had big plans for his first real home. "He had lived in base housing for 18 years and any home was a dream home to him," said his mother, Ernestine.

Tapley and his wife, Yi, bought the three-bedroom house in 1989. He wanted to build a patio and spend more time with sons Allen, 13, and John, 10. And he wanted to grow things. "He loved flowers, especially roses, and was planning a garden," Yi said.

After Tapley's death Feb. 6 in a helicopter accident, the family was deluged with flowering plants. First into the garden was a red rose bush sent by Tapley's aunt.

JAMES DAVID TATUM, 22
Army Spec.; Athens, Tenn.

Friends — who called him David — say Tatum was an artist.

"He was especially good with his hands," recalled retired McMinn County High School teacher Rhodelle Cunningham. He was good at basket-weaving, silk-screening, and "he weaved the bottom of chairs for friends of mine," she said.

Tatum also had simple tastes: "He liked home-made biscuits and saw-mill gravy," said his father.

In his final letter home, Tatum, who died in the Feb. 25 Scud missile attack, wrote: "No war is right, but if it is God's will, I will do everything I can do for the cause."

PHILIP JESSE "JAY" THOMAS, 25
Navy Petty Officer; Chapel Hill, N.C.

An only child, Thomas was his dad's "best friend." They built model airplanes together and stayed in close touch during Thomas' six and a half years in the service. When on leave, father and son would camp on the Outer Banks of North Carolina or fish Albemarle Sound. They exchanged fishing tackle every Christmas.

"He was a giver, not a taker, and he and I had a special relationship," said his father, Phil Thomas, director of the North Carolina Firefighters Association. The younger Thomas, an aircraft technician, died Dec. 30 in a vehicle accident.

JAMES K. THORP, 30
Marine Capt.; Valley Station, Ky.

"He loved flying and couldn't believe the Marines were paying him to do something that he would have done for nothing," said his father, William. Thorp died Feb. 2 with three other Marines when their helicopter crashed.

DONALDSON P. TILLAR III, 25
Army 1st Lt.; Miller School, Va.

Tillar was a graduate of the U.S. Military Academy, where he was a member of the lacrosse team. His father, a retired Army colonel, served in Vietnam and was an administrator at West Point. Tillar was one of eight members of the 1st Aviation Regiment who died Feb. 27 when their helicopter was shot down by Iraqi troops.

STEVEN R. TRAUTMAN, 21
Army Spec.; Houstonia, Mo.

Though not eager to serve in the gulf, Trautman thought it would be "a new challenge, a new excitement." The helicopter mechanic was fatally injured Feb. 26 when struck by a helicopter blade. Trautman's mother had lost her first husband in Vietnam, and his father was wounded in action there, losing a leg.

ROGER E. VALENTINE, 19
Army Pvt.; Memphis, Tenn.

Valentine went to the gulf one month after his wedding. He died three days after the cease-fire was declared.

His sister said he would have preferred going to college, but his family couldn't afford to send him. Nevertheless, he was proud to be a soldier. "I am in good health and hanging in there," he wrote to his sister. "The first cavalry will kick butt and then come home and tell the stories."

Valentine was either killed by Iraqi fire or by a land mine — his family said they received conflicting reports.

MARIO VEGA-VELAZQUEZ, 35
Army Sgt.; Ponce, Puerto Rico

A collector of Star Trek toys, Vega-Velazquez was a mechanic with the 160th Special Operations Aviation Regiment. He died Feb. 22 when a helicopter, helping transport wounded soldiers, crashed in rain and fog. "He was a good soldier and he loved the Army," said his sister, Milagros Gonzalez. "He helped other people that were in trouble, and that makes us feel really good."

SCOTT N. VIGRASS, 28
Army Pvt.; Tonawanda, N.Y.

Vigrass got married June 17 and left for the gulf on Aug. 21. His wife, Lisa, was expecting a baby in April. "He wanted me to have this baby in case he didn't return," said Lisa. Before he left, Vigrass said to her, "What if I never come home? What if I never come back?" The truck he was driving overturned Dec. 8.

CARPIO VILLARREAL, JR., 55
Air Force Senior Master Sgt; San Antonio, Texas

Villarreal was about to retire from the Air Force reserves, but he volunteered for one last mission. He had accumulated 6,300 flying hours with the 68th Military Airlift Squadron of the 433rd. He died in the late August crash of a transport plane in Germany.

ROBERT VOLDEN, 38
Navy Petty Officer; New York, N.Y.

Volden wanted to settle down in the Blue Ridge Mountains. "He always had this dream of having a country place, with land. He figured the Navy was a career where he could retire as a young man," said his uncle Arthur Rauscher, who raised Volden since age 3. Volden was killed in a boiler accident aboard the USS *Iwo Jima* on Oct. 30.

ROBERT CURTIS WADE, 31
Army Pfc.; Savannah, Ga.

The last time Doris Wade heard from her only child, Robert, he talked fast. He was in a hurry, just having been assigned to a unit. Only hours later he was dead — the victim of the Feb. 25 Scud missile attack in Dhahran. Known to family and friends as Curtis, Wade was a long-time baseball fan who starred on his Little League team and played second base in high school. "It won't be a hard job remembering him," said his mother. "Everybody who knew him loved him."

JAMES ERIC WALDRON, 25
Marine Lance Cpl.; Jeannette, Pa.

Care-free, easygoing Waldron was changed by the war. He was still the family's curious, laid-back youngest child, but he was growing up. "You could see it in his letters, even in his pictures," said sister Yvette. "There was such a difference. He was maturing."

Waldron wrote to everyone who wrote him, including a high school special-education class. In his letter, he wrote: "I'm sorry I rambled on a bit much. I hope this isn't for a grade."

When Waldron first went to the gulf, he said, "I'm not a hero. I'm just someone who wants to come home,'" recalled Yvette. He died Feb. 26 during a Marine assault at the Kuwait International Airport.

CHARLES SCOTT WALKER, 19
Army Pfc.; Jonesboro, Ga.

Walker and his brother, Martin, were both stationed in the Persian Gulf. After Walker, a scout with the 3rd Armored Division, died Feb. 1 when his gun accidentally discharged, his brother returned home on 30-day leave to be with their mother.

DANIEL B. WALKER, 20
Lance Cpl.; Whitehouse, Texas

Walker was killed Jan. 29 in the border skirmish near Khafji. Along a half mile of Corey Street, where his family lives, mailboxes, trees and telephone poles were covered in yellow ribbons. The funeral was held in his high school gymnasium. Walker's father said, "Daniel went about his life with purpose, resolve, and an impeccable heart."

FRANK J. WALLS, 20
Army Spec.; Hawthorne, Pa.

Walls once thought he'd pursue a career in law enforcement. But when he discovered he had problems with color blindness, he switched to engineering and joined the reserves. "Between the reserves, college and taking care of his dad, who was in the hospital, Frank was a busy young man," says stepfather Ted Minich. Walls died in the Feb. 25 Scud missile attack.

DIXON L. WALTERS, JR., 29
Air Force Capt.; Navarre Beach, Fla.

Walters was a certified public accountant for one year, but was truly bored, said Kim, his wife and college sweetheart. In the Air Force, Walters found a career full of excitement. When not playing with his two young children, the triathlete fit in 40 to 50 mile bike rides. Walters was aboard an Air Force AC-130 gunship that crashed Jan. 31. Listed as MIAs, all 14 crew members were believed to be dead.

BOBBY M. WARE, 21
Army Spec.; New Bern, N.C.

"I just think my son died for a useless cause," said his mother, Thelma, after learning her son had died when his jeep collided Jan. 20 with a heavy equipment transporter.

DAVID WARNE, 28
Navy Lt.; Jacksonville, Fla.

Warne had been stationed for only 10 months at Cecil Field Naval Air Station, Fla., where he was a member of the Strike-Fighter Squadron 86. His F/A-18 Hornet crashed Jan. 12 into the Mediterranean Sea during night training off the USS *America*.

BRIAN P. WEAVER, 22
Navy Petty Officer; Lockport, N.Y.

The former Eagle Scout joined the Navy to see the world. He visited Australia and Africa. He climbed Mount Fuji in Japan. He fought a fire that killed three servicemen on the aircraft carrier USS *Midway*. On Dec. 23, he died when his tour bus overturned near Abu Dhabi, the capital of the United Arab Emirates.

PAUL J. WEAVER, 34
Air Force Maj.; Navarre Beach, Fla.

Listed as MIA, he was a crew member of an Air Force gunship that crashed Jan. 31. All crewmen are believed to be dead.

TROY WEDGWOOD
Army Spec.; The Dalles, Ore.

Wedgwood, who drove towing equipment, was killed March 4 when he stepped on a land mine. He is survived by his wife, Tammy, who grew up two streets away from Wedgewood and was a high school classmate.

LAWRENCE N. WELCH, 41
Army Sgt.; Chisholm, Minn.

Welch was looking to the future. He planned to marry Patricia Tasson when he returned to the States. He was studying accounting when his National Guard unit was activated. "The loss of Larry [who died of heart failure] really doesn't make sense at times," said Pastor Steve Breitbarth of Grace Lutheran Church. "Larry visited with me before leaving. He had mixed feelings, but he was proud he could serve our great country."

SCOTTY LYNN WHITTENBURG, 22
Army Sgt.; Carlisle, Ark.

He was like thousands of other young men from a "rural town in the farming South, with a fishing pole and a Bible," said his father, Billy. A favorite family photograph shows a pint-size Scotty and older brother William in their "little Army uniforms."

"He wore it until he could only wear the shirt. Then only the hat," said the elder Whittenburg. "His ambition was to be an Army person."

A laser technologist, Whittenburg died Feb. 27 in Saudi Arabia when a cluster bomb exploded in the hands of a nearby soldier.

His father feels "no remorse about the incident. I grieve for the family of the young man that was standing nearby."

DAVID MARK WIECZOREK, 21
Army Pfc.; Gentry, Ark.

At the local grocery store, where Wieczorek worked after graduating from high school, he kept customers laughing with imitations of Gomer Pyle, the fictional television Marine created by Jim Nabors, said Jim Twiggs, who hired Wieczorek when he was 15.

"He didn't have a father, and I just kind of filled that void for him," Twiggs said. "His mother died [shortly before his high school graduation] and we just kind of adopted him. He just kind of worked his way into our lives. I guess because I didn't have any sons, he just filled that void for me."

Wieczorek died March 1, a day after stepping on a cluster bomb in Iraq.

JAMES N. WILBOURN III, 28
Marine Capt.; Huntsville, Ala.

"Trey" Wilbourn showed a great respect for George C. Patton. The Army general's photo hung in his bedroom; the *Patton* movie theme song motivated him before high school football games. Wilbourn was the public informa-

---

tion officer for his squadron and filed dispatches for the Cherry Point, N.C., base newspaper. The pilot's plane crashed Feb. 23 during a combat mission.

JAMES WILCHER, 25
Army Sgt.; Crystal Springs, Miss.

The poem he wrote and sent to his mother, Beatrice Wilcher, for her birthday was the last correspondence she received before he died Nov. 8. An electronics technician, Wilcher apparently died of natural causes in Saudia Arabia.

PHILIP L. WILKINSON, 35
Navy Petty Officer; Savannah, Ga.

The 13-year veteran helped manage the mess hall aboard the carrier USS *Saratoga*. Called "Levi," he was a native of Nevis, West Indies, and went to high school in St. Croix, Virgin Islands. He died December 22 when a ferry returning sailors from shore leave capsized in the choppy Mediterranean Sea.

JONATHAN M. 'JOE' WILLIAMS, 23
Army Cpl.; Portsmouth, Va.

Williams hoped one day to own a beauty shop with his mother. He'd run the business; she'd style hair. Williams entered the military to help pay for college, which he enrolled in after his tour ended. Reactivated, he died in the Feb. 25 Scud missile attack on his barracks. "He told us, 'I don't want to go, but I'll do what I have to do,' " recalled his mother, Carrie Caldwell. "If I don't make it back, I'll go to a better place."

COREY L. WINKLE, 21
Army Pfc.; Lubbock, Texas

Winkle was a theater-arts major at Texas Tech University. Soon after enlisting in August 1989, he received a notice to audition for a part in the Walt Disney movie *White Fang*. Said theater professor George Sorenson, "He had an incredible ability to surprise with something spontaneous onstage."

Winkle died Feb. 25 when a grenade accidentally exploded.

BERNARD SEAN WINKLEY, 27
Marine Chief Warrant Officer; Windsor, Maine

"I don't want to give my son. I don't want to give anybody's son, but freedom is not free and somebody has to pay for it," said his father, Henry, after learning that his son had died Feb. 8 in a tank accident during a dust storm near the Kuwait border.

HAROLD P. WITZKE III, 28
Army Staff Sgt.; Caroga Lake, N.Y.

A nine-year veteran and an M-1 tank crewman, Witzke was killed Feb. 26 by enemy fire in Kuwait. The Army called him "an exceptional soldier," and awarded him numerous service commendations. He leaves a wife and two children.

RICHARD V. WOLVERTON, 22
Army Spec.; Latrobe, Pa.

"Rick wore his heart on his sleeve, and what you see was what you got," said his mother. "He was always there when his friends needed him." He died Feb. 25 in a Scud missile attack.

JAMES E. WORTHY, 22
Army Spec.; Albany, Ga.

He was a straight-A student, basketball player and a member of the fashion board at Albany (Ga.) Technical Institute. Friends said he was a ham in front of a camera. He was released from the active Army in August. His reserve unit had been in Saudi Arabia only a week when an Iraqi Scud missile leveled his barracks.

KEVIN E. WRIGHT, 23
Army Cpl.; Louisville, Ky.

He was killed March 2 when a trash fire spread and ignited ammunition in Iraq. Wright never saw his daughter, Devin Noelle, who was born after he left in September. The girl will "probably go through a part where she won't understand, but then she'll be proud," his wife said.

THOMAS C.M. ZEUGNER, 36
Army Maj.; Petersburg, Va.

Zeugner was an explosives expert in the gulf. Before the war, he worked in counter-terrorism and special security. He had traveled with various secretaries of state and accompanied President Carter to Israel.

And he had a soft side. John Zeugner called his brother, the godfather of three, "extremely generous;" each year Zeugner gathered canned goods from friends to give to villagers he met during his fishing trips to Baja California.

The ultimate tribute, however, is how his buddies felt about him. "When he was being sent over to Saudi Arabia," said brother John, "we heard some men who had previously served with him volunteered to go over with him. That's how much they respected him."

Zeugner is survived by his mother and two brothers. The Army said he died of a gunshot wound to the head; the death is under investigation.

Missing in action

Listed as missing in action, as of March 8.

PATRICK K. CONNOR, 25
Navy Lt.; Virginia Beach, Va.

Connor's attack bomber was downed over Iraq Feb. 2.

BARRY T. COOKE, 35
Navy Lt. Cmdr.; Virginia Beach, Va.

The father of three was shot down over Iraq Feb. 2 during a bombing run.

WILLIAM T. COSTEN, 27
Navy Lt.; St. Louis, Mo.

Costen, who has a physics degree, is a triathlete and steeplechase runner, and likes to build furniture. His A-6 bomber was shot down Jan. 18.

DONNIE R. HOLLAND, 42
Air Force Maj.; Bastrop, La.

Holland, a teacher before he joined the Air Force at age 25, flew an F-15E fighter-bomber that was shot down by Iraqi fire Jan. 18.

THOMAS F. KORITZ, 37
Air Force Maj.; Rochelle, Ill.

The high school football star is one of only five Air Force pilots/surgeons. His F15-E Eagle was lost Jan. 18.

STEPHEN RICHARD PHILLIS, 30
Air Force Capt.; Rock Island, Ill.

He was listed missing Feb. 15 when his A-10 Warthog jet went down during a bombing run. "(Stephen) believed in what he was doing, and he loved what he was doing, so I have no regrets," said his mother, Diane.

MICHAEL SCOTT SPEICHER, 33
Navy Lt. Cmdr.; Jacksonville, Fla.

Speicher was the first U.S. flier listed as missing and is presumed dead. His F/A-18 was lost the first night of the war. His father was a World War II flier.

DAVID SPELLACY, 28
Marine Capt.; New River Air Station, N.C.

He was the forward air controller on an observation plane that went down Feb. 25.

CHARLES J. TURNER, 29
Navy Lt.; Oak Harbor, Wash.

Helene Turner said her son enjoyed spending time with his brother at their northern Minnesota hunting camp. A navigator, his bomber was lost Jan. 18.

REGINALD C. UNDERWOOD, 33
Marine Capt.; Havelock, N.C.

Before heading overseas in August, Underwood and his wife settled on a boy's and girl's name for the child to be born during his absence. He saw photos of daughter Anne before the jet he piloted was downed Feb. 27.

CHAPTER 7
The Feel of Victory

The victory in the gulf was swifter and far less costly in American lives than any of the nation's nine previous wars — including the Spanish-American War, in which U.S. forces won every battle. Never had so much been accomplished with so few deaths.

Yet, in its excitement, the nation was reminded of what one American mother — Dorothy Walker Bush — had told her son: To gloat in success is not to succeed at all.

George Bush remembered that advice when he declared on Feb. 28 that the war was over. "Kuwait is liberated. Iraq's army is defeated," Bush told the nation. "This is not a time of euphoria, certainly not a time to gloat. But it is a time of pride — pride in our troops, pride in our friends who stood with us in this crisis, pride in our nation."

For President Bush, victory in the gulf brought a wave of public support unheard of in decades — and gave him new political strength to tackle problems at home and pursue a lasting peace in the gulf. For the U.S. military, victory in the region erased the lingering self-doubts of a nation which remembered too well the pain of Vietnam.

For the American public, victory touched off an explosion of patriotism, and a new feeling of confidence in the nation's economic and military might. As President Bush said, "The brave men and women of Desert Storm accomplished more than even they may realize. They set out to confront an enemy abroad and, in the process, they transformed a nation at home."

And for the soldiers who fought the war, victory meant the end of life in a bleak desert and a trip back home. Going home. For weeks, for months, the promise sustained U.S. troops.

They didn't fight just for parades, medals, promotions or bragging rights. They didn't endure terrifying desert nights, lonely boring days and the realities of war just to prove how tough they were. They did it for the first kiss of a loved one, their children's smiles as they were swooped into tight hugs — and much more.

Army Staff Sgt. Bruce Friedrichs, 35, of Fort Stewart, Ga., had a special motivation for hurrying home. His son Robert John, 8, has cerebral palsy and has been confined all his life to a wheelchair. But while Dad was gone, young Robert learned to get around using a walker. "I expect him to walk — for the first time — into my arms," said Friedrichs.

Air Force Lt. Col. Don Kline, 42, of Dallas, couldn't wait to hold his two young sons in his arms. An F-15 pilot and commander of the 27th Tactical Fighter Squadron, he had missed both boys' birthdays. But Kline said he had another reason for wanting to go home: to say "thank you" to the people whose support buoyed him and his men during the war. "The real heroes of this conflict," he said, "are the American people."

In the days after the war was declared over, U.S. troops in the Persian Gulf spent much of their time getting ready to leave. It was a time for packing, for scouring the marketplaces for souvenir T-shirts and tacky camel figurines, for saying goodbye to comrades staying behind and mourning those who went home in caskets. Soldiers wondered how to find the right words to explain everything they saw, felt and did. They worried that loved ones would see in their eyes the new hard edge that only war can create. "I'm worried about how it'll be when I walk off the plane," said Army Spec. Jonathan Harrell, 29, of Alexander City, Ala. "I keep telling myself they haven't forgotten me."

Some made sacrifices to the end. Air Force Sgt. Frank Hosselkus volunteered to stay longer so married colleagues could go home first. "It's hard, especially today, seeing a lot of guys out-process and get ready to go," he said. "It's more important for the married guys to get home." Hosselkus, 22, a munitions officer from Pevely, Mo., will spend his six weeks of waiting making plans to buy some rural Florida property. "When my time comes to go home, I'll be ready."

Army Command Sgt. Maj. Wallace Hunter was so fired up about going home to Nashville that he didn't know how he would stand the two-week wait.

"I can't wait to get out of this place. Enough is enough. U.S.A., here I come!"

The Staff

The stories in this book were gathered from USA TODAY reporters around the world — Laurence Jolidon, Judy Keen, Paul Hoversten, and Kurt Spitzer in Saudi Arabia, Richard Price and Bill Nichols in Israel, Marilyn Greene in Kuwait, Don Kirk and Johanna Neuman in Iraq, and Jack Kelley in Jordan.

Book editors: Joe Urschel, Amy Eisman, David Colton, Adell Crowe, Chris Fruitrich.

News editors/writers: Dennis Cauchon, Steve Davis, Mindy Fetterman, Gwen Flanders, Susan Goldberg, Debbie Howlett, Tim Kenny, William Nicholson, Andrea Stone, Bob Twigg, Ed Wells, Michael Zuckerman.

Book contributors: Laurel Adams, Robert Barbrow, Mary Ellin Barrett, Marty Baumann, Ben Brown, J. Taylor Buckley, Anne Carey, Anne Davis, Chris Donahue, Denny Gainer, Barbara Hansen, Michelle Healy, Carol Herwig, Shawn McIntosh, JoAn Moore, Martha T. Moore, Jim Myers, Jim Norman, Brian O'Connell, Barbara Pearson, John Riley, Anita Sama, Jim Schulte, Eugene Sloan, Patricia Stang, Tracy Walmer, Larry Weisman and Tish Wells.

— Julia Wallace, Managing Editor/Special Projects
— Tom McNamara, Managing Editor/News